GREAT ARCHITECTURE

OF MICHIGAN

GREAT ARCHITECTURE OF MICHIGAN

TEXT BY **JOHN GALLAGHER**

PHOTOGRAPHS BY **BALTHAZAR KORAB**

MICHIGAN ARCHITECTURAL FOUNDATION

 Michigan
Architectural
Foundation

Michigan Architectural Foundation

553 East Jefferson Avenue

Detroit, Michigan 48226

313.965.4100

www.michiganarchitecturalfoundation.org

Design: Savitski Design, Ann Arbor, Michigan

Printing: University Lithoprinters, Inc., Ann Arbor, Michigan

Bindery: Dekker Bookbinding, Grand Rapids, Michigan

Digital Mastering of Images: Christian Korab

Production Manager: Sandra Knight Pogue

ISBN 978-0-9816144-0-3

To my parents, Helen and John, and to my wife, Sheu-Jane

— John Gallagher

For Monica my wife and Christian my son, who were
invaluable help with this significant book

— Balthazar Korab

CONTENTS

FOREWORD

Senator Carl Levin

The state of Michigan, almost entirely surrounded by the world's greatest fresh waters, has one of the most distinctive and easily recognizable boundaries on the planet. But the state's geography is just one of the forms that has shaped Michigan's story of growth and production. Another enduring backdrop is the buildings that have housed some of Michigan's finest moments, with architecture that is as diverse and eclectic as the people of Michigan. *Great Architecture of Michigan* is a wonderful depiction of Michigan's rich history of innovative design and construction, opening the doors of our architectural past so that it can be appreciated by future generations.

As this book brilliantly illustrates, architects of local and world renown have spread their talents across the state, with many designs that are worthy of recognition. Each period of Michigan's development is reflected in its buildings, from the open countryside dotted with simple farmsteads and elaborate Victorian and Greek revival farmhouses, to the historic cities characterized by streamlined Art Deco industrial structures and bold machine-age complexes. Human stories are showcased in the buildings within these pages, from the Point Betsie Lighthouse that guided ships up and down Lake Michigan to the Ford River Rouge Plant that produced cars for the masses. The plant was also an integral part of the "Arsenal of Democracy" that helped win World War II, and was a defining site of the American labor movement.

Through its impressive photography, informative text, and colorful design, *Great Architecture of Michigan* provides a creative portrayal of structures that span Michigan's storied history and geography. The featured buildings reflect the practicality, optimism, and spirituality of Michigan's people. This wonderful book will enlighten and impress Michigan residents and nonresidents alike with a vast array of architectural styles, where they can be found in Michigan, and how they relate to the shared story of humanity's connection to Michigan's two pleasant peninsulas.

CELEBRATING MICHIGAN'S ARCHITECTURE

John Gallagher

Walk, jog, bicycle, or motor through any corner of Michigan, no matter how rural or remote, and you'll find great architecture at almost every turn. Iconic buildings lend character throughout the state: the Grand Hotel on Mackinac Island, the State Capitol in Lansing, the Guardian Building in Detroit. There are hundreds more buildings less well-known but equally meritorious. They define our towering cities and our smallest hamlets. Some of these buildings were new when Abraham Lincoln was practicing law; others went up so recently that the paint has hardly dried. Stylistically, they represent every school and period, from Greek Revival and Queen Anne to Art Deco and International Modern. Taken all in all, they are Michigan's past and its future, its heritage and its promise.

This book celebrates that great architecture. We present 150 of the state's best buildings, with photographs by Balthazar Korab and text by myself, the architecture critic of the *Detroit Free Press*. This is your Michigan. These buildings, though mostly privately owned, belong to all of us, for they form the common cultural inheritance of our state.

Flip through these pages and be amazed at the range, the depth, and the quality of Michigan's architecture. See, for example, Parkwyn Village, a cluster of homes by Frank Lloyd Wright in Kalamazoo, built in the 1940s in a sympathetic nod to community living. Marvel at the sturdy elegance of the Point Betsie Lighthouse. Contrast the ornate Beaux Arts elegance of the Ryerson Library in Grand Rapids with the sleek modernism of William Kessler's Detroit Receiving Hospital. See how civic pride created noble city halls and courthouses in Bay City, Crystal Falls, Houghton, and Lapeer. Lumber and copper fortunes in the 19th century left a legacy of great houses and libraries in Muskegon and the Upper Peninsula just as automotive fortunes in the 20th century did the same in Detroit. But these are just a few examples among many.

This book grew out of an effort by the non-profit Michigan Architectural Foundation to celebrate the foundation's 50th anniversary in 2007. The foundation directors asked a five-member jury, headed by Eric J. Hill, FAIA, professor of the practice in architecture at the University of Michigan Taubman College of Architecture and Urban Planning, to make the 150 selections. Besides Korab and myself, the other jurors were Kathryn Bishop Eckert, former state historic preservation officer and author of the encyclopedic book *Buildings of Michigan*, and Anthony Martinico, professor of architecture at the University of Detroit Mercy.

Five judges different from the ones who chose the 150 buildings portrayed here may have included some other selections; indeed, that is highly probable, given the subjective nature of aesthetic choices. But everyone would agree that the 150 buildings presented here offer a representative sample of Michigan's greatest work.

We present these buildings through the lens of Balthazar Korab, the dean of America's architectural photographers. Trained as an architect in his native Europe, Korab settled in the Detroit area and turned to photography full time in 1960. His work in these pages spans his career and represents the output of several decades. That being so, some of the photos here depict a building that has since undergone restoration or additions, like the Battle Creek Station or Orchestra Hall in Detroit. Indeed, readers familiar with specific buildings may be able to date one of Korab's photos to the 1970s or '80s or '90s from the visual clues in the image. We made no effort to re-shoot the 150 buildings anew as of 2008, when this book was created, for this book is as much a record of Korab's vision of Michigan's architecture, of what he saw and captured during his long career, as of the buildings themselves.

The difference between a Korab portrait and a snapshot that the tourist takes often is the difference between seeing a building with full understanding and not seeing it at all. Study Korab's perfectly composed photograph of McGregor Memorial Conference Center and see how the master captures

Photographer Balthazar Korab, left,

with author John Gallagher

the tranquility and harmony that is the essence of Minoru Yamasaki's design. Or turn to Korab's portrait of the Honolulu House in Marshall, warmed by the sun's glowing rays, to see what ordinary shutterbugs miss.

With each building, we list four identifying elements: name, address, date, and architect. Bear in mind that the names by which buildings are known can change with new owners and new uses, and that listing the main architect or firm does not always capture the contribution of everyone who worked on a design. Indeed, many of our projects (especially those a century or more old) have been touched in the ensuing years by many architects; each through their careful work helped the building survive and continue to be a valuable part of Michigan's architecture heritage. To try to name each and every firm or architect that worked on a historic building would be unwieldy, and in many cases impossible given the incomplete records. If one restoration architect is named for a particular historical project, such as Richard Frank for the Michigan State Capitol, it is because the restoration rose to a level that redefined the building or so enhanced its value that it all but demanded recognition. But by not naming the numerous architects who have worked on these many buildings, we mean no slight. Rather, we simply wish to smooth the reader's path with the most pertinent and essential facts.

As for dates, architecture is not instant art. We have tried to list a date for each building that reflects when the building was completed, dedicated, first occupied, or otherwise went into service. Construction may have started years earlier, and later renovations or additions may have altered the appearance of a building significantly. To the extent that other reference works may opt to present some of these buildings under different dates (or alternate names, architects, and even addresses) that represents differences of opinion or emphasis, not mistakes.

This book tells several stories, and one of them is about survival. A number of our 150 buildings faced the wrecking ball, and not a few survived only because dedicated individuals rallied like-minded citizens at a crucial time. Today it's hard to overstate the importance of Orchestra Hall in Detroit to the city's renaissance, yet that great building was almost lost. So, too, were the Bay City Hall, the Traverse City State Hospital, the David Mackenzie House, the Andrus House, and the Elwood Bar & Grill, among others shown in these pages. Their crime was often nothing more than being out of style as tastes changed, or standing in the way of a sewer line or gas station. Yet all those once-threatened buildings now serve as anchors of their communities. We urge the preservation of these (and other) buildings not for the sake of nostalgia alone. Michigan's stock of historic buildings is proving crucial for the dollars-and-cents revitalization of our state.

Once published, books tend to enjoy a life of their own, and we hope this book will endure as long as some of the buildings it portrays. It may be that visiting businessmen or diplomats will carry home a copy of *Great Architecture of Michigan* to Munich or Tokyo or Seoul, delighting readers far and wide. This book may turn up on the shelves of school libraries in Flint and Benton Harbor and Dearborn, inspiring some young man or young woman to take up architecture as a career (or photography or writing, for that matter). It could serve as a travel guide for rambles about the state. Best of all, we hope this book opens minds to the thought that Michigan's finest days are still ahead. No one can browse through the glorious record captured in these pages, marveling at the energy and the creativity, and not believe that Michigan still has more to give.

1 BUILDINGS WE GATHER IN

Grand Hotel

Mackinac Island

1887

George Mason
of Mason and Rice

When the Grand Hotel opened at the height of the Gilded Age, it joined many other historic resort hotels across America. Today it remains one of the few survivors, and without doubt one of the best. Architect-builder Charles W. Caskey executed the plans drawn up by Detroit architect George Mason, and everywhere we see Mason's sure hand and eye for detail. The slender columns that frame the great porch, the rounded ends of the veranda that soften what might otherwise be severe straight lines, and the open central belvedere that punctuates the skyline all attest to Mason's skill. Can there be a grander spot to enjoy a summer morning or to survey the vistas of the Straits of Mackinac? A Michigan masterpiece in every way.

Point Betsie Lighthouse

Crystal Lake north of Frankfort

1858, 1880s–90s additions and renovations

Architect unknown

Blessed with more than 3,000 miles of coastline, Michigan once lit its shorelines with one of the nation's most impressive collection of lighthouses. Modern navigation technology rendered many obsolete, but the historic Point Betsie Light, overlooking Lake Michigan at the entry to the Manitou Passage, still shines. It evokes the best of the Michigan character: Sturdiness, reliability, and an unselfconscious elegance. Note how the impressively simple brick tower joins its Dutch-inspired house in a harmonious whole. The Point Betsie Light was automated in 1983, and today is undergoing renovation by volunteers.

Gandy Dancer
(Michigan Central Railroad Depot)

401 Depot Street, Ann Arbor

1886

Frederick H. Spier of Spier and Rohns

In our hectic age, travel may no longer represent the ceremonious pleasure it once did. But at least we have buildings like Ann Arbor's Michigan Central Depot to remind us of that earlier age. Built in the sturdy Romanesque Revival style popularized by architect Henry H. Richardson, the station evokes power and prestige through its deep-set round-arch openings, the sturdy massing of gables and tower, and the superb use of the native granite fieldstone. Refitted in modern times as the Gandy Dancer restaurant, the station has lost none of its nobility. This is one for the ages.

McGregor Memorial
Conference Center

Wayne State University Campus, Detroit

1958

Minoru Yamasaki

This jewel-like building, a ceremonial gathering spot on Wayne State University's campus, shows the genius of Minoru Yamasaki at its zenith. As with the best of Yamasaki's work, there is the elegance, the simplicity, and the sense a viewer gets that building and site were made for each other. Note the careful repeated use of diamond patterns, a Yamasaki motif here and elsewhere to mark entrances and central spaces. During a long career, Yamasaki produced many notable designs, in settings as varied as the sands of Saudi Arabia and the concrete canyons of lower Manhattan. But nowhere did he show greater assurance and mastery of his art than here in his adopted home of Detroit.

Walter and May Reuther
UAW Family Education Center

Black Lake near Onaway

1967–70

Oskar Stonorov

Every architect dreams of a great client. In long-time United Auto Workers President Walter Reuther, architect Oskar Stonorov found the client of a lifetime. Converting a secluded hunting and fishing camp to an education center, Reuther urged Stonorov to harmonize the buildings with the natural landscape, and he allowed only the bare minimum of tree cutting. Stonorov responded with some of his best work, blending Douglas fir, cedar, red birch, and teak woods, limestone from Wisconsin, and great panels of glass into a composition that is warm, open, and inviting. The entire complex, more than 1,000 acres in size, contains about 20 separate buildings, but so carefully did Reuther and Stonorov plan that all enjoy views of the streams and ponds.

Battle Creek Station

55 West Van Buren Street, Battle Creek

1888

Rogers and MacFarlane

Korab's photograph represents more than a snapshot in time of the old depot. His photo so captured the noble qualities of the station that local preservationists rallied to restore the building. Thanks to that restoration, visitors today can enjoy this interesting variation on the Richardsonian Romanesque style in all its glory. Note how the station features red brick and Lake Superior sandstone instead of the darker and heavier masonry more common to other 19th century depots. The dramatic upward thrust of the clock tower punctuates the otherwise low-lying horizontal plane. Note the overhanging eaves: Then as now, stations were built to keep passengers out of the rain. Although a building of its own time, the simple geometry and absence of ornament seem to hint at a more modernist aesthetic.

McMorran Place

701 McMorran Boulevard, Port Huron

1960

Alden B. Dow

Named for the business and political leader whose family donated the money to build it, McMorran Place has long served as a community anchor for Port Huron. Here in the center's multiple venues you can find concerts, ice hockey, political oratory, school graduations, theatrical shows, and so much more. The great Alden B. Dow, a landmark Michigan modernist, crafted a clean, mostly unadorned exterior and an orderly progression of spaces on the inside. But it's the limestone wall facing Huron Avenue that is particularly striking. Sculptor Marshall M. Fredericks designed the heroic figures dubbed Night and Day and the 22-foot-diameter sunburst clock.

Niles Station

598 Dey Street, Niles (above)

1892

Frederick H. Spier and William Rohns

In a state dotted with memorable train depots, this one in southwestern Michigan was designed to be a stand-out. As the final Michigan stop on Chicago-bound trains on the old Michigan Central line, the depot featured a kitchen and dining room, offices and apartments, all enclosed in a picturesque Richardsonian Romanesque composition that breathes strength and dependability. Still in use by Amtrak, the Niles Station has played bit roles in Hollywood movies, including *Continental Divide* with John Belushi and *Midnight Run* with Robert DeNiro.

Union Depot

610 West Western Avenue, Muskegon (opposite)

Opened 1895

Sidney J. Osgood

A small-town train depot takes on fairy-tale proportions in this picturesque composition by architect Sidney J. Osgood. The great squat tower could be a samurai castle, the baby turret at its side fit for a maiden's rescue, and the deeply recessed entry within the massive Romanesque arch a dragon's lair. Businessmen in late 19th-century Muskegon commissioned this beauty and lavished no end of care on it inside and out, including bronze and steel grillwork and great ornamental fireplaces. But who knew that so businesslike an enterprise could echo so romantically down the years? Retired in 1970, the station is now a local visitors center and museum.

The architect William B. Stratton was a devoted supporter of the Arts and Crafts movement, but late in his career he began to edge toward a modernist aesthetic. Here, he gave the Women's City Club an unadorned facade and slightly abstract massing. Yet his belief in handcrafted excellence shows in the superb brickwork and in the extensive use throughout the building of Pewabic tiles produced by his wife, Mary Chase Perry Stratton. The building was notable for social reasons, too: In the 1920s, Detroit's many women's organizations commissioned Stratton to design a meeting place for them, and in its heyday, the City Club eventually enrolled over 8,000 Detroit women in its classes and extensive recreation programs. Today the building figures in plans for downtown revitalization.

Women's City Club

2110 Park, Detroit

1924

William B. Stratton

Chicago Club

300 Chicago Avenue, Charlevoix

1881

Architect unknown

Flag-bedecked and brilliant in the summer sunlight, the Chicago Club captures the easy charm of a northern Michigan resort. Built as a summer getaway by members of a Chicago church group, the clubhouse still sports its wrap-around verandas and its stick-style ornamentation. Simple yet elegant, catering to successive generations of families, this is the sort of place you catch up with old friends, wile away the hours on the porch with a good book, and enjoy a community meal in the evening in the large dining room.

2 | BUILDINGS WE PLAY IN

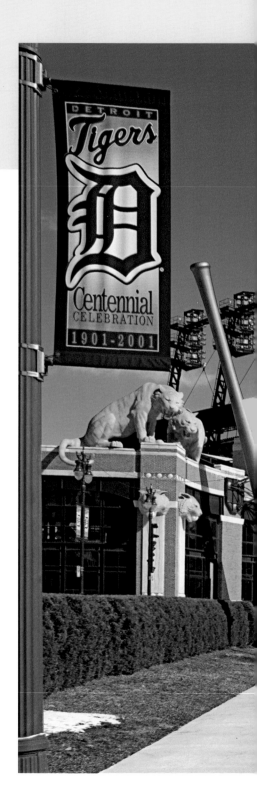

Comerica Park

Bounded by Witherell, Brush, Adams,
and Montcalm in Detroit
2000
HOK Sports and SmithGroup

This replacement for the beloved Tiger Stadium at Michigan and Trumbull had a tough act to follow. But the new stadium works: views are flawless from all over the ballpark, and the downtown Detroit skyline looms impressively over the outfield fences. Designers (working closely with the Ilitch family of pizza, theater, and sports fame who own the Tigers) added a distinctly Detroit entertainment flavor to the notion of updating historic ballpark architecture. Ball-eating tigers and giant baseball bats decorate the exterior, and everything from the enormous scoreboard to the amusement-park rides proclaim this a playground for young and old alike.

Van Andel Arena

130 West Fulton, Grand Rapids

1996

Rossetti Architects

Built as part of Grand Rapids' downtown revival, the Van Andel Arena (named for one of the founding families of Amway) offered a bracing shot of modern design to what had been a mostly traditional cityscape. Civically as well as architecturally ambitious, the arena with its winged roofline and shimmering curved front façade proclaimed that any notion of decline downtown was history. And, indeed, since Van Andel Arena began hosting sports and entertainment events, downtown Grand Rapids has enjoyed a string of other thoughtful modernist designs, including a new art museum and the DeVos Place convention center. Thus architecture became a key player in urban revitalization.

Ford Field

Bounded by Brush, Adams, I-375, and Montcalm in Detroit

2002

Rossetti Architects, SmithGroup

Unlike all the concrete bowl stadiums built in suburban cornfields, Ford Field tucks itself neatly into its urban setting downtown. The profile is lower than expected, as the architects recessed the playing field and many of the 65,000 seats below grade. Perhaps most intriguing, the stadium incorporates the old Hudson's retail warehouse along its southern edge, offering room for luxury suites overlooking the field and rental office space. The mostly brick exterior conveys a warm, traditional feel, while the signature rounded glass entry became an instant landmark. A focal point of activity during Lions games and special events, Ford Field solves several problems at once, including how to be a massive modern stadium yet contribute to a downtown revival at the same time.

Coleman A. Young Community Center

2751 Robert Bradby Drive, Detroit (above)

1981

William Kessler and Associates

Architecture serves the people in many ways, here as a recreation center in the heart of inner-city Detroit. The swimming pool area is delightfully bright beneath a rounded, frosted-glass curtain wall; the gym areas are spacious and efficient. And the design that achieves all this is deceptively simple. What appears at first to be a purely functional structure emerges on closer viewing as a careful study in geometry and massing. As this center shows, a tight budget in a struggling city doesn't preclude fine architecture.

Greektown

Monroe between Beaubien and St. Antoine and environs, Detroit (opposite)

Various dates beginning in mid-to-late 1800s,

Multiple architects and builders

Anyone who doubts that urban vitality lies in preserving older, human-scale buildings need only visit Greektown to be convinced. This collection of humble, Victorian-era commercial structures, mostly brick and two-to-four stories tall, has evolved over time into one of Detroit's liveliest tourist destinations. The first floors of most buildings house restaurants and bakeries, while some truly notable works of architecture, like St. Mary Catholic Church, anchor the district. The creation of Greektown Casino in the late 1990s added a new (some say overwhelming) presence—the latest chapter in a neighborhood that began as pioneer farm, morphed into a German and then a Greek enclave, and today pulses to the beat of urban entertainment.

Superior Dome

Northern Michigan University, Marquette

1991

CRS Sirrine and TMP Associates

The Upper Peninsula's long, harsh winters called for an indoor football stadium, but Northern Michigan University got much more than that when the Superior Dome opened in 1991. The world's largest wooden dome rises 14 stories and encompasses five acres within it. The roof can withstand tremendous winds and snow loads, thanks to the 781 Douglas Fir beams and more than 100 miles of fir decking. With the world's largest retractable turf floor, the Superior Dome hosts NMU's football Wildcats, as well as a lively mix of regional field hockey, soccer, trade shows, community events, even exercise walks by the locals, who have affectionately dubbed the place the Yooper Dome.

Cranbrook Natatorium

Cranbrook Educational Community, Bloomfield Hills

2000

Tod Williams Billie Tsien Architects

In the 50 years after Eliel Saarinen designed his last building at Cranbrook, the private school did little to update its campus. Then, in the 1990s, a burst of creativity saw five major new buildings built, of which the swimming facility, or natatorium, ranks as perhaps the best. The husband-wife team of Williams, a Cranbrook graduate, and Tsien crafted an exquisite interior that ingeniously aids heating and cooling with a pair of cylinder-like openings, or oculi, in the ceiling, and vertical baffles along the walls that can be opened and closed as needed. The pinpoint lighting pattern on the ceiling has been left random to mimic a night sky, and the pool surface flanks a curtain wall that offers views of the wooded landscape outside. Both functionally and visually, this is a champ.

Belle Isle Conservatory

Belle Isle, Detroit

1904

Albert Kahn

Built to evoke the majesty of the turn-of-the-century City Beautiful movement, the conservatory echoes earlier conservatories, including one at the World's Columbian Exposition in Chicago. With its huge central glass dome and its symmetrical glass wings, the conservatory houses a bountiful collection of plants from around the world and remains a popular visitors' spot on Belle Isle to this day. The conservatory marked an early success for young Albert Kahn, who was demonstrating here and elsewhere that he could tackle any commission with ease and grace. The conservatory was simplified during a later reconstruction, but it retains its power and elegance.

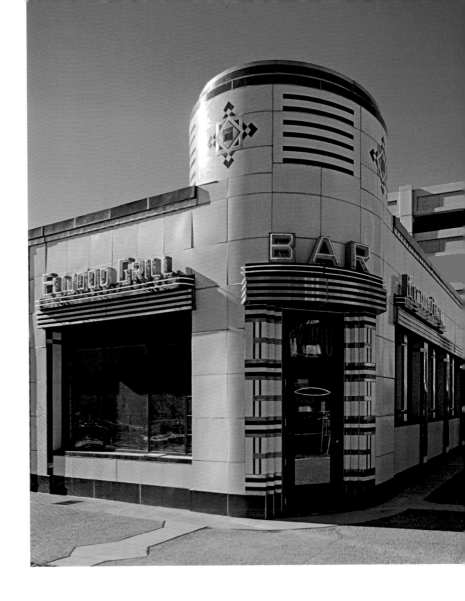

Elwood Bar & Grill

Brush and Adams, Detroit

1936; relocated 1997

Charles Noble

Good things come in delightfully small packages. This lively little gathering spot gives a human touch to Detroit's theater-stadium district and remains the city's best-known example of the streamlined Art Moderne style. The enameled steel panels and rounded corners look as fresh today as when first built. Note the geometric decorative patterns on the tower and the colorful signage. Originally built at Elizabeth and Woodward (hence the "El" and "Wood" of its name), it was moved in the late '90s to make way for the new Tigers and Lions stadiums. Today it stands just outside the entrance to both, draws huge crowds on game days, and remains one of Detroit's great architectural "saves."

3 BUILDINGS WE GOVERN IN

Michigan State Capitol

Bounded by Capitol, Walnut,
Allegan and Ottawa, Lansing
Completed 1878, dedicated
Jan. 1, 1879; restored 1990s
Elijah E. Myers; restoration
Richard C. Frank

Large and majestic, the great Michigan State Capitol is more restrained than, say, the U.S. Capitol in Washington, D.C. Its Neoclassical exterior is rather more simple, its marvelous dome more slender. Yet the Michigan Capitol remains one of the nation's finest state capitols, especially among the survivors of the great period of civic architecture in the Victorian era. The more opulent interior borrows freely from classical and High Victorian motifs, and, thanks to the 1990s restoration, shines in all its glory. Architect Elijah Myers went on to design state capitols in Texas and Colorado, making him one of our most important, if relatively unknown, civic architects.

Keweenaw County Courthouse

5095 4th Street, Eagle River

1866, 1925

J.B. Sweatt (original)

This dignified seat of criminal justice began as a simpler building but in 1925 was revised into the classical form we see today. It has the look of a traditional New England meeting house. When even a small rural community in the far reaches of the Upper Peninsula creates so lofty a work, it testifies to the civic pride, architectural ambition, and craftsmanship found throughout Michigan.

Calumet Village Hall & Theater

340 Sixth Street, Calumet

Village Hall 1885; opera house 1900

J.B. Sweatt and Charles K. Shand

Built in two stages, first a village hall followed in a few years by the much larger opera house, each designed by different architects, the Calumet Village Hall & Theater remains an Upper Peninsula glory. The style evokes the Italian Renaissance Revival, but the use of local red sandstone on the lower exterior, and copper from nearby mines on the upper reaches, makes this a distinctly local interpretation. The gorgeous theater inside, which now seats 700, is a marvel that serves as a cultural and social anchor for its community.

Bay City Hall

301 Washington Street, Bay City

1897

Leverett A. Pratt and Walter Koeppe

One glance at Bay City's magnificent city halls tells you why the Romanesque Revival style popularized by H.H. Richardson became the mode of choice in late 19th century America. The double-arched entrance, the deeply recessed windows, the clock tower soaring some 180 feet, and the multiple gables projecting from the red-tiled roof all convey a spirit of endurance and sturdy elegance. The interior is no less fine, with a grand atrium and ornate stairways worked in cast iron and trimmed in Victorian floral design. What a treasure! Yet a study once urged its demolition in favor of something more modern and up-to-date. That idea thankfully went nowhere.

Kalamazoo City Hall

241 West South Street, Kalamazoo

1931

Weary and Alford

In the 1930s, architects often updated the classical style with streamlined Art Deco imagery to produce a particularly appealing type of government building. Here, Chicago architects Weary and Alford decorated their limestone façade with tall fluted pilasters and relief panels showing both historical scenes and floral and geometric patterns. The framing of the recessed windows are of dark cast aluminum. The interior includes a three-story atrium. Simple yet elegant, this building evokes a dignity appropriate to civic democracy.

Wayne County Building

600 Randolph Street, Detroit

1896–1902

John Scott; restoration by Quinn Evans Architects

and Smith, Hinchman & Grylls in the 1980s

Built with pre-automotive fortunes when Detroit was just coming into its own, the Wayne County Building aimed at — and hit — a goal of being among the most sumptuous buildings in Michigan. An outstanding example of Beaux-Arts Classicism, it features four stories of Ohio sandstone surmounting a rusticated granite base. Baroque sculptural elements pierce the skyline, and a slim yet elaborate tower emphasizes the lofty ideals of a free people. From the monumental stone staircase leading to a pavilion with Corinthian colonnade to an interior enriched with many types of domestic and imported marbles, this remains one of Michigan's architectural masterpieces.

Governor's Summer Residence

Fort and Spring Streets, Mackinac Island

1902

Frederick W. Perkins

One might argue that a summer cottage doesn't belong with other buildings of government. But this beautiful example of Shingle-style resort residence is all business when the governor — any governor — is politicking legislators, reporters, or business tycoons. Lawrence Young, a Chicago lawyer and railroad man who helped develop the Grand Hotel, built this for himself, and designer Perkins gave it all the touches that raise it above the ordinary. Rugged native limestone boulders form the base as well as the chimneys, the huge hipped roof sports flaring eaves and projecting dormers, and the cozy porch wraps around most of the structure. The State of Michigan bought the house in the 1940s. Take the weekly tour in summer, or wrangle an invitation from the governor, and you get to enjoy spectacular views of the Straits of Mackinac.

Saginaw County Castle Building

500 Federal Avenue, Saginaw

1898

William M. Aiken

Michigan does not boast a wealth of French Chateau style architecture, but what it has tends to be first rate. This fairy-tale edifice began life as a post office. In an inspired move, the federal government at the time required its new civic buildings to reflect the heritage of local communities. So architect William M. Aiken drew on a French historical style in a tribute to the region's early white settlers; he also noted that the corner towers suggested a defensive fort in frontier days, while the decorative carvings evoked native plants and wildlife. Having twice escaped the wrecking ball in the 20th century, the building survives in a modified but handsome style today as a local historical museum.

Marquette County Courthouse

234 West Baraga Avenue, Marquette
1904 (restored mid-1980s)
Demitrius F. Charlton and R. William Gilbert;
restoration Lincoln A. Poley

This impressive courthouse on a bluff sloping down to Lake Superior tells two stories, really. One is of the willingness of turn-of-the-century citizens to tax themselves to build this monument to civil order and justice. The other is of how American architecture so often mixes and matches styles and materials in a delightfully original way. Here, a building with clear classical roots is clad in North County red sandstone; the cornice is copper (no surprise in a copper-mining region); the massive red granite columns came from Maine; and the interior sports Italian marble and fine hardwoods. Fans of the movie *Anatomy of a Murder* may spot the courthouse in a few scenes.

Tuscola County Courthouse

440 North State Street, Caro

1933

William H. Kuni

This Depression-era courthouse shows the blending of classical style with a pared-down modern aesthetic. There is the mere suggestion of columns in the fluted pilasters separating the tall round-arched windows at the entrance, and florid classical ornament gives way to a restrained decorative banding carved into the limestone exterior. Known variously as "stripped classicism" and "Depression modern," the style proved dignified and well-suited to government buildings. The architect, William H. Kuni of Detroit, also designed the Alpena County Courthouse just after this, and the two buildings could be siblings.

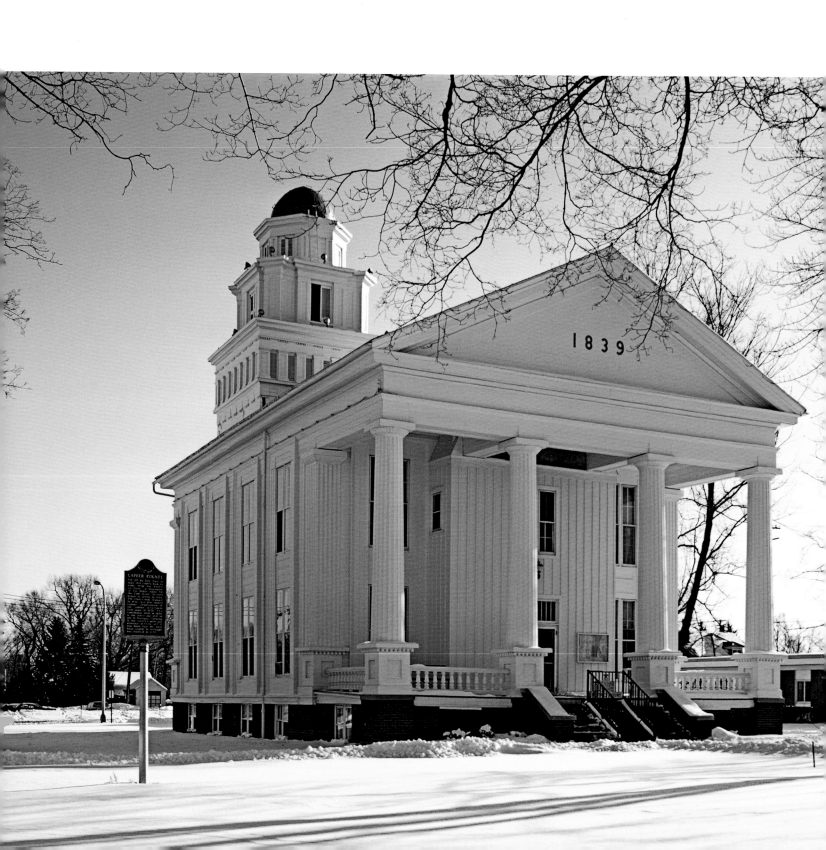

Lapeer County Courthouse

Courthouse Square, Lapeer

1845–46

Alvin N. Hart

Builders on the rawboned frontier often turned to classical styles to achieve a sort of ready-made grandeur. This oldest surviving courthouse in Michigan still in active use presents a dignified example of Greek Revival architecture. The massive portico has four fluted Doric columns supporting the pediment. The elegant tower to the rear, three-tiered and tapering to a small dome, adds further embellishment. The exterior is of native white pine on a brick foundation. With such monumental and stately architecture, early Michiganders built cities in the wilderness. One footnote: The date in the pediment, 1839, commemorates the construction of the county's first courthouse, not this building itself, which came in the mid-1840s.

Iron County Courthouse

2 South Sixth Street, Crystal Falls

1891

J.C. Clancy

Located on a commanding bluff offering panoramic views, the majestic Iron County Courthouse is among the most notable structures north of northern Michigan. Architect J.C. Clancy worked in the Romanesque Revival style favored then for many civic buildings, but the impressive arrangement of towers and turrets, and the outstanding stone and brick work, reflect local pride as much as European antecedents. Victorian-era Americans often expressed civic pride through their architecture, but seldom did they produce an example so grand.

Frank Murphy Hall of Justice

1441 St. Antoine, Detroit

1968

Eberle M. Smith and Associates

The term Brutalist architecture derives from a French phrase meaning "raw concrete" and not, as its critics claimed, from the style's perceived arrogance and coldness. Even so, many untrained eyes may see something alien and unapproachable in this striking tower. But look closer. See how the vertical slabs and delineated sections express in a no-nonsense manner the internal scheme of courtrooms, detention facilities, and offices. And observe how, some 40 years after it opened, the structure still projects a bracing clarity and efficiency. Alien? Perhaps. But a good building, all the same.

Houghton County Courthouse

401 East Houghton Avenue, Houghton

1887

J.B. Sweatt

This fanciful Gothic-inspired edifice looks almost too playful for the serious business of jails and courts. Located high on a bluff overlooking Portage Lake, the courthouse features a mansard roof covered in beautifully weathered copper from local mines. The bands of red trimming over the windows, which help to visually unite the building, are local sandstone. The multi-colored variety is enhanced by the use of buff-colored brick, unusual in this type of setting. The picturesque tower, the roof dormers, and a variety of trimming add to the medley. Expanded and renovated over the years, and still a beauty.

Alpena County Courthouse

720 Chisholm Street, Alpena

1935

William H. Kuni

Fresh from designing his quite similar Tuscola County Courthouse, William H. Kuni crafted this even more restrained example of Depression modern. The structure made use of a then-novel poured-concrete product, while the interior shows Art Deco imagery, including zig-zag and chevron motifs and geometric patterns in the terrazzo floor. Like the best of government architecture from that era, the courthouse is simple, dignified, utilitarian, even, perhaps, beautiful — a worthy example of democratic ideals given shape in steel and concrete.

4 BUILDINGS OF THE ARTS

Detroit Institute of Arts

5200 Woodward Avenue, Detroit

1927

Paul Philippe Cret, with multiple

additions and renovations by others

The DIA ranks among the world's great museums and stands as an undisputed giant on the Michigan architectural scene. Architect Cret was born in France and brought a classical training to his commission here. The Renaissance-inspired look and the clear, logical arrangement of galleries around the central great hall proved so convincing that the *Encyclopedia Britannica* then used the layout to illustrate the ideal museum. Over the years, north and south wings were added amid multiple renovations and expansions, including a thorough internal reordering completed in 2007. But Cret's original still commands pride of place, a masterpiece where millions of Detroiters first learned about art.

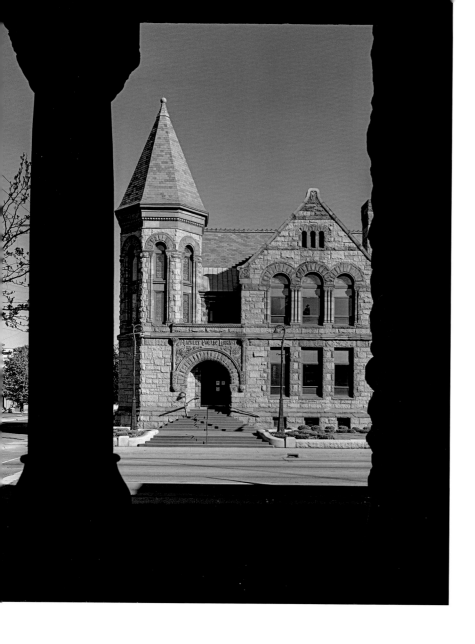

Hackley Public Library

316 West Webster Avenue, Muskegon

1890

Normand S. Patton

Lumber baron Charles Hackley, one of the wealthiest men in America, gifted this sturdy stone structure to his adopted home. The deep-cut arched entrance, the octagonal tower, and the large gable on the upper level all contribute to an impressively solid composition. Compare and contrast this with the Grand Rapids Public Library elsewhere in this book. Both are examples of millionaires' gifts that took different stylistic paths to the same end of public-spirited generosity.

Hill Auditorium and Burton Memorial Tower

University of Michigan campus, Ann Arbor

1913 (Auditorium) and 1936 (Tower)

Albert Kahn

Two more gems from the team headed by Albert Kahn, Hill Auditorium and Burton Memorial Tower to this day remain icons of the UM campus in Ann Arbor. The auditorium, recently restored, offers a large performance hall with world-famous acoustics, while the Burton Memorial Tower vies with Michigan Stadium to be UM's most famous and photographed structure. That Kahn's firm got so many important commissions testifies to his skill; from auto factories to concert halls to office towers to private homes, he could do it all.

Holocaust Memorial Center

28123 Orchard Lake Road, Farmington Hills

2003

Ken Neumann of

Neumann Smith & Associates

The symbolism here is not meant to be comfortable. Barbed-wire-like cable wreaths the center. A symbolic guard tower evokes menace. And vertical stripes stir uneasy memories of prisoner garb at places like Auschwitz, where Nazis murdered millions of Jews. The interior tells an even more powerful story. After a final, almost sunny reminder of pre-World War II life in a Jewish village in Europe, a visitor winds down ramps and hallways deeper into the darkness of Nazi horrors. Finally, daylight returns with the emergence into a post-war chamber of remembrance. Architect Ken Neumann said he left the historical wounds as raw as possible, as a cry for tolerance and as a stark reminder of past crimes against humanity.

Power Center for the Performing Arts

121 Fletcher Street, Ann Arbor

1971 plus 1981 addition

Kevin Roche, John Dinkeloo and Associates;

addition Jickling, Lyman and Powell

The Power Center looks so new and fresh that it's hard to believe it's almost 40 years old at this writing. University of Michigan regents commissioned Kevin Roche and John Dinkeloo, protégés of the great Eero Saarinen, to design this music and stage center, and they delivered in style. Supporting columns on the exterior stand slightly apart from the structure as if giving it room to breathe. The glass curtain wall at night transparently reveals the glowing lobby within. The stage area itself is technically a marvel, with an orchestra pit that rises to create a thrust stage. Who's the star here? Maybe the building itself.

The Henry Ford

Village Road and Oakwood Boulevard, Dearborn

1929; various additions

Robert O. Derrick

Dedicated in 1929, the museum known now as The Henry Ford was designed to house its namesake's immense collection of Americana. With Ford's blessing and encouragement, architect Derrick made faithful reproductions of Independence Hall in Philadelphia as well as the neighboring Congress Hall and Old Philadelphia City Hall. Just steps away, Ford laid out his Greenfield Village, several dozen originals or reproductions of historic buildings. Taken together, this enormous assemblage of historic architecture remains a cultural touchstone and one of Michigan's most visited sites.

Cranbrook Museum and Library

39221 Woodward Avenue, Bloomfield Hills

1942

Eliel Saarinen

Toward the end of his long association with the Cranbrook campus, the great Finnish architect Eliel Saarinen pared down his folk-inspired, multi-layered style to an almost abstract modernism. The result was the composition that, more than any other, defines not only Cranbrook but the zenith of Michigan architecture for many people. Almost always photographed with either the Triton Pool or the Orpheus Fountain by Carl Milles in the foreground, the Museum and Library vista remains the incomparable Cranbrook shot and an inspiration to generations of visitors.

Michigan Theater

603 East Liberty, Ann Arbor

1928

Maurice H. Finkel

Early Hollywood moguls didn't seem to realize that what they put on the silver screen provided escape enough for patrons; instead they built theaters to evoke a fantasy world even with the lights on. So, long before the advent of the suburban multiplex, Americans paid their pennies at downtown movie palaces like this one. Thanks to ongoing care and strong community support, it remains an anchor for its community.

This major addition to Detroit's Cultural Center is the largest African American historical museum in the country and a destination for visitors of all races and ethnic backgrounds. Created by one of the city's most important African American architecture firms, the museum features abundant African design imagery, including columns based on a traditional African rope motif. The central hall contains many other symbolically important decorative elements and has been the site of numerous important gatherings, including a public wake for civil rights pioneer Rosa Parks.

Charles H. Wright
Museum of African American History

315 East Warren Avenue, Detroit

1997

Sims-Varner

Detroit Public Library Main Branch

5201 Woodward Avenue, Detroit

1921; later additions

Cass Gilbert; additions by Cass Gilbert, Jr.

and Francis Keally

Generations of Detroiters have trekked to the Main Library on Woodward, checking out the latest mystery or thriller, tracking down ancestors in the old files, or researching scholarly work on everything from folk dancing to Urdu. The main branch could not have served so many for so long had not the talented Cass Gilbert, later architect of the U.S. Supreme Court in Washington, D.C., not done such a fine job creating it. From the quiet but impressive front façade to the vaulted hall and expansive reading rooms on the upper floor, the library remains the perfect place to wile away a lunch hour, complete a school paper, or nail down an elusive fact. Facing the Detroit Institute of Arts across Woodward, the library forms one half of Detroit's great architectural duo.

Grand Rapids Public Library
(Ryerson Library)

111 Library Street, Grand Rapids

1904

Shepley, Rutan and Coolidge

Today communities pay for public libraries mainly by selling bonds, but during the Gilded Age, multimillionaires, most famously Andrew Carnegie, donated them to a grateful public. Here, Grand Rapids native Martin A. Ryerson, a prominent Chicago businessman, graced his hometown with this temple of knowledge. Befitting Ryerson's lofty intent, the style is Beaux-Arts Classicism, the feeling formal and dignified. In our own more recent time, downtown Grand Rapids has added many modernistic buildings to its cityscape. But Ryerson's gift holds its own amid changing tastes as an exemplar of Old World generosity and public spirit.

Detroit Masonic Temple

500 Temple, Detroit

1926

George Mason

Nearly 40 years after he designed the Grand Hotel on Mackinac Island, Mason crafted this incredibly fine blend of Neo-Gothic imagery and the modern tall building. The public is most familiar with the main theater, a large venue for music, drama, civic celebrations, and numerous other events. Tucked away upstairs are a number of smaller but equally distinguished rooms for the Masonic rites. The entire structure is believed to be the largest Masonic temple in the world and possibly the most beautiful. Mason lived into his 90s and graced Michigan with many fine buildings. Certainly this one, done at an age when most men are retired, deserves to be ranked among his best.

Fox Theatre

2111 Woodward Avenue, Detroit

1928; restored 1988

C. Howard Crane; restoration

William Kessler and Associates

The legendary Fox is perhaps Detroit's most exotic architectural setting. Like other great movie palaces of the 1920s, it gave generations of Detroiters a fairy-tale setting in which to find entertainment, drama, or merely an escape from reality for a couple of hours. This opulent mélange of Egyptian, Hindu, Persian, Chinese and Indian motifs was lovingly restored in the late 1980s when the Ilitch family of pizza, sports, and entertainment fame bought it. Since then, the Fox has anchored downtown's revival and served as cornerstone of the city's theater and stadium district.

Hoyt Public Library

505 Janes Avenue, Saginaw

1890

Van Brunt and Howe

Named for the wealthy business family that built it for the city as a gift, Hoyt Public Library grew out of a design competition that featured entries from some of America's greatest architects, including McKim, Mead and White of New York and H.H. Richardson of Boston. The winners, Van Brunt and Howe of Boston, endowed the building with a Romanesque exterior, large limestone blocks, red sandstone trim, intersecting dormers, arched entrance, and other touches that spoke of durability and stability. The interior was finished in oak. Over time, renovations and additions bruised the gentility, as when the oak woodwork was painted instead of refinished, but a recent renovation has restored the original luster inside and out.

Orchestra Hall

3711 Woodward Avenue, Detroit

1919

C. Howard Crane; restoration by Quinn Evans Architects and Richard C. Frank

The great theater architect C. Howard Crane, who went on to craft the Fox and other movie palaces in Detroit, did this job in a rush under threat of losing Detroit Symphony conductor Ossip Gabrilovich unless a proper home for the DSO was built. And so the exterior looks a little boxy, the Neoclassical ornament applied rather perfunctorily. No matter. The interior hall is an acoustical and artistic marvel, and a fitting home for one of the nation's great ensembles. Incredibly, this landmark faced the wrecking ball in 1970, but was saved and restored under the loving hand of noted preservation architect Richard C. Frank. Here, too, we see Korab capturing a building at a moment in time, for the steel framework to the right became the new Max M. Fisher Music Center, of which Orchestra Hall is the most important part. Thus Korab demonstrates that architecture, however solid and formal, changes with the years just like people do.

William L. Clements Library

909 South University Avenue, Ann Arbor

1923

Albert Kahn

Architect Albert Kahn garnered his greatest fame for his innovative factories for Henry Ford. But gazing at this exquisite small library on the University of Michigan campus, one gets the distinct impression Kahn felt most comfortable amid the splendors of old Europe. The delicate tripled-arched entrance, formed by the two slender Corinthian columns, shows a true mastery of the late Italian Renaissance forms that inspired him here. Built to house the collection of American manuscripts bequeathed to UM by William L. Clements, this was said to be Kahn's personal favorite of all his many buildings, and it's easy to see why.

Cranbrook Educational Community

39221 Woodward Avenue, Bloomfield Hills
1907; 1918–42; 1990s
Eliel Saarinen, multiple others

It's not just the individual buildings, many designed by the great Eliel Saarinen, that make Cranbrook so memorable. It's the whole package — buildings, gardens, fountains, outdoor sculpture, landscape design — that have earned Cranbrook international fame. One need not attend one of Cranbrook's schools (elementary, secondary, or post-college graduate programs) to savor the splendor. A day spent strolling the grounds reveals the essence: that Cranbrook is a place where beauty reigns; where every window sash, table lamp, bookshelf, and flower vase reflects a craftsman's care and love. Many architects contributed, but pride of place must go to newspaper publisher George Booth, one of Detroit's great art patrons, who bought this rolling farmland early in the 20th century and spent the rest of his life building and shaping it.

Cranbrook School

39221 Woodward Avenue, Bloomfield Hills

1927

Eliel Saarinen

Cranbrook School was Eliel Saarinen's first building in America, and he modeled it after a medieval college, with classrooms, dormitories, and dining hall grouped around a multilevel courtyard. Already, though, we can see the synthesis that marked Saarinen's greatest work, an adherence not to any one period or style, but a creative blending of medieval motifs, Scandinavia folk styles, and an Arts & Crafts sensibility. Much admired elsewhere, this was the first building to win Cranbrook lasting fame. Here as elsewhere on campus, ornamentation and outdoor sculpture by many different artists contribute handsomely to the overall effect.

Kingswood, Cranbrook's school for girls, nestles along the edge of a small lake with a wooded hillside as backdrop. One of Saarinen's most evocative designs, the copper roof, overhanging eaves, and strikingly original Art Deco motifs have combined to make Kingswood one of Cranbrook's most photographed buildings. And here, too, we see the full flowering of the Saarinen family genius: Eliel designed the building, his wife, Loja, the rugs, drapes, and fabrics, daughter Pipsan some of the interiors, and son Eero, who one day would loom hugely over American architecture, crafted the furniture.

Kingswood School

39221 Woodward Avenue, Bloomfield Hills

1931

Eliel Saarinen

Cranbrook Institute of Science

39221 Woodward Avenue, Bloomfield Hills

1938

Eliel Saarinen; Stephen Holl

The most visited of Cranbrook's buildings, the science institute is really two structures in one, the original by Saarinen and a larger wing designed by Stephen Holl in the 1990s. For his part, Saarinen showed a transitional style here, an essay in horizontal lines and flat roofs that is about halfway between his richly detailed Kingswood School of a few years earlier and the even more pared-down modernism of his later Museum and Library. Holl's addition, modestly tucked away behind Saarinen's original, is more about handling big crowds and thus less evocative; it includes a 42-foot tall "light laboratory" in which different colored and shaped pieces of glass reflect sunlight in ever-changing ways.

Kettering Campus Center

Kettering University, Flint

1969

TMP Associates

From its founding in 1919 as a night school for engineers, Kettering University (formerly called the General Motors Institute) has never wavered from its role as a training ground for "the alpha-gearhead, the mathlete, the future CEO." The campus center building that opened in 1969 gave bricks-and-mortar form to that ideal. Heavily influenced by the thoughtful modernism that Eero Saarinen practiced in the 1950s and early '60s, the center's low slung silhouette was a far cry from the Collegiate Gothic style prevalent on so many other campuses. Stripped of historical imagery, and benefiting from the latest in technology, the student center was a place for the serious work of science and engineering. It still is today.

Law School Quadrangle

University of Michigan, Ann Arbor

1924–33

York and Sawyer

The style known as Collegiate Gothic, borrowed from Oxford and Cambridge to lend weight and authenticity to numerous American schools, was seldom employed to finer effect than here. Four distinct buildings were planned and built around the central quad, and the effort proved so successful that a library extension added many years later was built underground so as not to spoil the effect. Everywhere the architectural detailing contributes to a feeling of awe and reverence, with a multitude of stone tracery windows, stained glass, oak paneling, busts, and carvings. The cathedral-like main research library remains one of Michigan's most regal rooms.

Nineteenth-century American architects often blended Old World styles to achieve something new and impressive. Here at Hillsdale College in rural southern Michigan, we find a conservative Italianate building gloriously topped by a French Second Empire roof. Not surprisingly, this great wedding cake of a building remains the focal point of the Hillsdale campus, and has symbolized the college and its values for decades. Hillsdale College, an independent liberal arts school with a student body of about 1,300, still uses Central Hall for many of its administrative offices, including Admissions, Financial Aid, and the Registrar.

Central Hall, Hillsdale College

Hillsdale College campus, Hillsdale

1874

Brush and Smith

Horace H. Rackham Building

915 East Washington, Ann Arbor

1938

William Kapp of Smith, Hinchman & Grylls

Simple yet majestic, the Rackham Building remains one of the most visited and admired buildings on the University of Michigan's central campus. A sort of all-purpose home for graduate studies, Rackham includes a 1,200-seat lecture hall and multiple music, study, meeting, and exhibition rooms. The style shows the restrained, pared-down classicism that was used to good effect on many government buildings during the Depression. The overall impact is greatly enhanced by its setting, recessed back from the street with a wide staircase leading up to the front entrance.

Fordson High School

13800 Ford Road, Dearborn

1928

H.J. Keough

When Fordson High opened in 1928, many people acclaimed it the most beautiful school in the state. Modeled in part after the then-new University of Michigan law school, Fordson is an impressive example of Collegiate Gothic, a style which adopted an Old World look to evoke a seriousness of purpose and dedication. The central entrance tower, faced with granite and sandstone trim, would not be out of place at Oxford or Cambridge. Among Fordson's many notable alumni have been former U.S. Senator Robert Griffin, Marian Ilitch of pizza and casino fame, and legendary United Auto Workers President Walter Reuther.

Cass Technical High School

2501 Second Avenue, Detroit

2005

TMP Associates

Cass Tech has long boasted of elite status among Detroit public schools, with a roster of grads that includes award-winning actresses Lily Tomlin and Ellen Burstyn and a bevy of police chiefs, mayors, artists, musicians, and sports figures. When the time came to replace its aging, Gothic-inspired building, the school boldly stepped into the 21st century with this sleek, efficient, and bracingly modern new home. Natural daylight spills in everywhere, and the multistory library and media center provides panoramic vistas of the city. With Detroit working to rebuild its central core, the new Cass Tech serves as an anchor for the north-west corner of downtown.

Lester K. Kirk Collegiate Center

Olivet College, Olivet

1962

Meathe, Kessler and Associates

A generation or two before, a student center might have been designed as a massive castle-like Romanesque building. But Harvard-trained modernist William Kessler shows his mastery of a lighter, more delicate, yet bracingly clean and efficient style. Notice how the building is slightly elevated, and how the thin support columns branch out to support the overhanging roof, both features that enhance the impression the center is almost floating in space. At night, the glass walls let the building glow from within. A focal point of campus life, the center houses dining rooms, bookstore, campus radio station, offices, and lounges.

Ann & Robert H. Lurie Tower

University of Michigan North Campus, Ann Arbor

1996

Charles W. Moore

As the University of Michigan burst the bounds of its central campus, it began to build many of its new facilities on a north campus a mile or two distant. The 165-foot Ann & Robert H. Lurie Tower creates an exclamation point for this north campus; it also provides a counterpoint to UM's more famous Burton Memorial Tower on the main campus. The Ann & Robert H. Lurie Tower at first glance seems more modern and streamlined than the Burton Memorial Tower, but look again. The copper roof and the veneer of bricks and ceramic tile evoke tradition as much as the future, although in a post-Modern accent to be sure.

Detroit School of Arts

123 Selden, Detroit

2005

Hamilton Anderson Associates

One of the flagship public schools in Detroit, this unique entity is as much performing arts center as classroom building. Production spaces include an 800-seat auditorium, 200-seat recital hall, black box theater, television and radio studios, art studios and galleries, vocal and instrumental music rehearsal rooms, and top-floor media center and dining hall. Located just steps from Woodward Avenue and the Max M. Fisher Music Center, the Detroit School of Arts is sending its talented graduates out to enrich the cultural life of the city and beyond.

Kresge-Ford Building, College for Creative Studies

245 East Kirby, Detroit

1975

William Kessler and Associates

A college devoted to teaching painters, sculptors, photographers, and other creative types their trade needs a building to inspire them. Architect William Kessler gave the school just that with this boldly new and different exploration of structure, form, and expression. The 32-foot modules were designed to be stacked and added to as more space was needed (although, once finished, the building did not grow beyond this initial phase). Derided by some as a mere Lego toy, the building for many others has become a modern icon and a lasting symbol of the school.

6 BUILDINGS WE WORSHIP IN

St. Francis de Sales Church

2929 McCracken, Muskegon

1966

Marcel Breuer with Herbert Beckhard

The internationally acclaimed mid-century modernist Marcel Breuer designed only a couple of buildings in Michigan, but this Catholic church in Muskegon ranks high among his world triumphs. Breaking the boundaries of acceptable religious architecture, Breuer let his concrete walls rise and twist into a geometric shape known as hyperbolic paraboloids; inside, vertical concrete ribs, stark and severe, rise heavenward behind the altar. The horizontal enclosure on top houses the suspended bells. This was something new in church design, yet appropriately spiritual. Perhaps a building in northern Michigan could hope for only so much fame; had this been built in, say, mid-town Manhattan, it would be as famous as any church in the land.

Congregation Shaarey Zedek

27375 Bell Road, Southfield
1962
Percival Goodman and
Albert Kahn Associates

Perhaps no house of worship in Michigan enjoys so dramatic a setting as Congregation Shaarey Zedek. Set on a bluff overlooking the juncture of Northwestern Highway, I-696 and the Lodge Freeway, it beckons to many thousands of daily commuters. Inspired by Frank Lloyd Wright's First Unitarian Meeting House in Madison, Wisconsin, Shaarey Zedek's dramatically upthrust sanctuary has been likened to a monumental Hebrew tent or tabernacle or, more abstractly, to the human spirit reaching heavenward. A stunning display of stained-glass windows makes the interior even more dramatic. There is a social story here, too: This is the seventh home of the conservative congregation that was founded in Detroit during the Civil War era and gradually moved northward as the city grew.

Saints Peter and Paul Church

629 East Jefferson Avenue, Detroit

1844–48

Francis Letourneau

The oldest surviving church building in Detroit, Saints Peter and Paul went up while Abraham Lincoln was practicing law and endures today in the age of the Internet. The style is closest to English Regency with classical motifs. St. Catherine's Chapel, built on the rear of the main church in 1918 in an architecturally sympathetic style, today serves as the parish administration center. One of the oldest buildings featured in this book, Saints Peter and Paul has served as a symbol of Roman Catholicism in the city for more than 150 years.

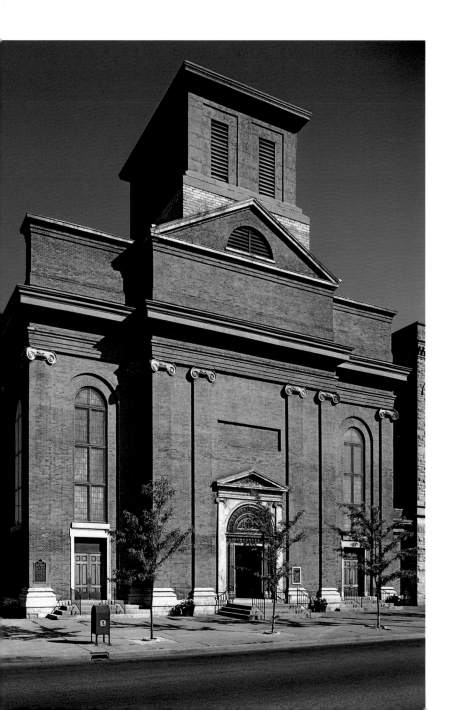

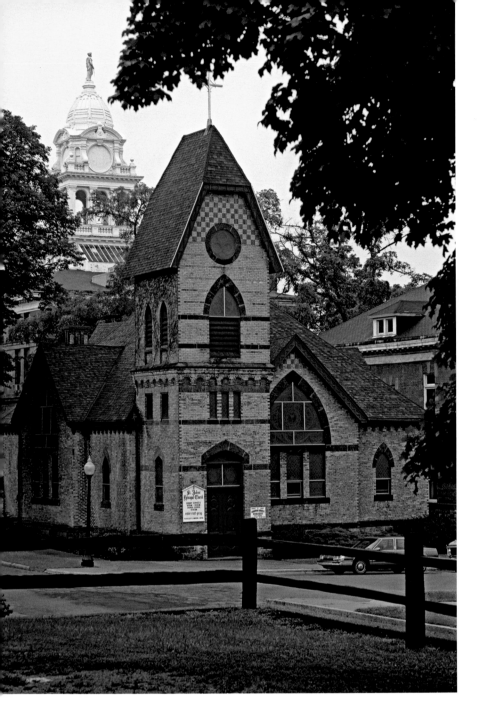

St. John's Episcopal

120 North Kidd Street, Ionia

1883

Orry Waterbury

Still think the Victorians were dull? Not when it came to their architecture. This picturesque Gothic church in western Michigan shows many of the delightful touches that marked the High Victorian style: varied-colored bricks used in checkerboard pattern and other ornamentation, and the theatrical cap known as a jerkinhead that tops the tower. The church has been a visual landmark in its community for more than a century. St. John's also hints at the talent of a local who never went beyond his chosen patch. Orry Waterbury spent a career in the vicinity designing all manner of buildings. What might he have accomplished given the opportunities of, say, an Albert Kahn?

Fort Street Presbyterian

631 West Fort Street, Detroit

1855

Octavius and Albert Jordan

Church spires dominated the skyline of pre-Civil War Detroit, and Fort Street Presbyterian survives from that period. A single glance reminds us of the pride and ambition, both civic and religious, of that bygone day. The style is a rather copiously applied Gothic Revival, with a myriad of details that include the almost impossibly slender spire; a small octagonal turret was modeled after a chapel at Cambridge University in England. The church suffered major damage in fires in 1876 and 1914 but was rebuilt both times virtually to the original plan. It stands today as a downtown landmark and a vibrant center of faith.

First Unitarian Church (Hobbs + Black)

100 North State Street, Ann Arbor

1882

Donaldson and Meier

This sturdy fortress-like church from the 1880s tells an important story — that a building built for one use can morph into something entirely new. Since 1985, the Hobbs + Black architectural firm has called this church home. The firm transformed the sanctuary into its light-filled production studio, restoring the wood trusses and leaving the church's original stone end walls exposed. A Tiffany stained glass window unexpectedly found within a sanctuary wall was restored and relocated to the lobby. Many original details were kept inside and out, creating a connection with the past. Without generous adaptive reuse like this, much of Michigan's architectural legacy would be lost.

St. Joseph's Catholic Church

1828 Jay Street, Detroit

1873

Francis G. Himpler

There are many varieties of Gothic Revival architecture; this Roman Catholic parish in central Detroit utilized the hall church model from southern Germany. Little wonder: The parish arose to serve Detroit's German population, and architect Himpler was Berlin trained. The workmanship is especially fine; the stained-glass windows are nationally recognized for their quality. The eight-sided bell house was added in 1883 and the impressive spire 10 years later. In a link to its heritage, the parish still offers a German-language Mass on the fourth Sunday of each month.

Trinity Episcopal

1519 Martin Luther King Jr. Boulevard, Detroit

1892

Mason and Rice

People who built Gothic Revival churches in America in the 19th century tended to trowel on the Gothic details in a fashion not historically accurate. Newspaper publisher James E. Scripps wanted to reverse this tendency toward fanciful gingerbread edifices. Paying out of his own pocket for an Episcopal church near his Detroit home, he engaged an English architect to study authentic models in Britain first, then had Mason and Rice work from his copious notes and drawings. The resulting style is a reflection of English Gothic from the late 14th century. Even the tracery in the windows is archeologically correct. The late architectural historian Gordon Bugbee dated the birth of Neo-Gothic revival church design in America to this building.

First Congregational
United Church of Christ

412 Fourth Street, Manistee

1892

William Le Baron Jenney and William Otis

Unlike a Gothic-style church with its slim spire, churches in the Romanesque mode tend to show corner towers that are square and solid. But seldom does this feature dominate its church, and the local skyline, like the massive tower of First Congregational in Manistee. Visible as a landmark from Lake Michigan, the bell and clock tower made absolutely clear that morality and decency would overcome sin and vice in this late 19th century lumber-industry town. Long after the White Pine industry left, the church endures. The interior is notable, too, with a cavernous yet dignified sanctuary, and two memorial windows crafted by Louis Comfort Tiffany.

Woodside Church

1509 East Court, Flint

1952

Eero Saarinen and Robert Swanson

A modern design seems appropriate for this multicultural, multi-denominational, socially active congregation in Flint. The church worked with groundbreaking modernist Eero Saarinen on the initial design and with Robert Swanson on the final, award-winning scheme. The mostly unadorned brick walls and carillon tower testify to the designers' modernist sensibilities. Yet the crafts tradition Saarinen and Swanson imbued during their formative days at Cranbrook showed up here, too. Many of the sanctuary appointments were handmade; the warmth and texture of the brickwork shows great care; and stained glass from the 1889 church facility was remounted in nine windows at the new building.

National Shrine of the Little Flower

Woodward and 12 Mile Road, Royal Oak

1931, 1936

Henry J. McGill

Politically as well as architecturally notable, this Roman Catholic church enjoys landmark visibility at one of the busiest intersections in the region. The tower came first in 1931; the much larger church there today opened in 1936. The elaborate Art Deco styling of the limestone tower features a monumental relief figure of Christ crucified as well as many other sculptural figures. The eight-sided church employed a central altar with encircling seating long before many other churches adopted the idea. There is seating for 3,000 beneath a tent-like roof of copper and nickel-chrome steel. In the 1930s, the church's long-time pastor, Rev. Charles Coughlin, broadcast radio sermons blasting international bankers, labor unions, Franklin Roosevelt, and Jews, before his bishop eventually silenced him.

Basilica of St. Adalbert

701 Fourth Street NW, Grand Rapids

1913

Henry J. Harks

German-speaking Poles who settled in Grand Rapids in the late 1800s built this magnificent example of Romanesque-style church architecture. The imagery is rich and complex, with hints of eastern European motifs and stained-glass windows that depict Polish saints. Note the large copper-covered dome over the crossing of nave and transepts; twin front spires, topped with domed cupolas, flank the impressive triple-arched entrance and the circular stained-glass window. The $150,000 in early 20th-century dollars it cost to build this represented a huge outpouring of support from the community. More than bricks and mortar, the architecture tells a story of commitment and enduring values.

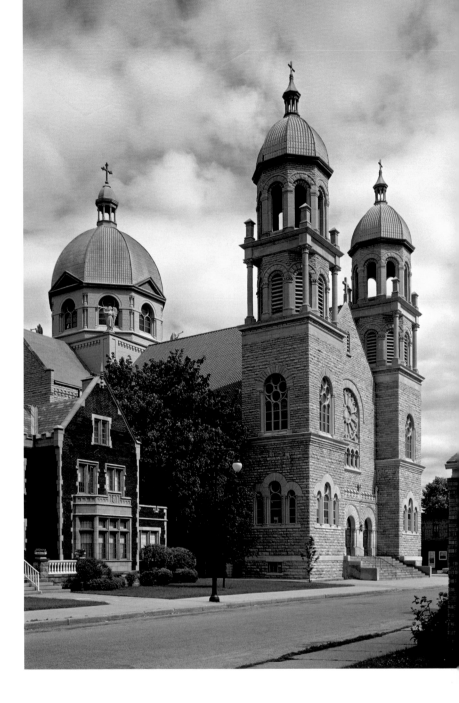

First United Methodist Church

315 West Larkin Street, Midland

1950

Alden B. Dow

In 1950, a long-time Methodist community opened this modern church to replace its older meeting house. Gone were the steeple, the Gothic imagery, and much of the other traditional look we've come to associate with church design. In their place, Alden B. Dow crafted a horizontal arrangement of brick planes topped by wide copper bands. The raised shrubbery bed and the stained glass add to the quiet dignity. On the interior, Dow's skillful use of high and low spaces contributes to an appropriate sense of the spiritual.

Christ Church Cranbrook

470 Church Road, Bloomfield Hills

1928

Bertram G. Goodhue Associates

Newspaper publisher George Booth, already hard at work developing his Cranbrook school, decided that a church was needed nearby for neighboring families. It's no surprise that he lavished the same care on this Episcopal structure that he did on his other projects. Numerous crafts masters contributed, including Pewabic Pottery founder Mary Chase Perry Stratton, who created the mosaics in the baptistery. Also notable are the wood carvings by John Kirchmayer, stained glass designs by G. Owen Bonawit, and the large fresco at the front of the church by Katherine McEwen. Perhaps more than anywhere else in Michigan, the church and nearby Cranbrook show the importance of the patron, and not just the architect, in creating beautiful buildings.

Calvary Baptist Church

1000 Robert Bradby Drive, Detroit

1977

Gunnar Birkerts and Associates

Wags may quip that innovative modernist Gunnar Birkerts produced a Howard Johnson's here and not a church. But there's no denying the power and originality of the form. The entire structure reaches heavenward and not just a steeple, and the dramatic orange color punctuates the otherwise traditional cityscape. Calvary Baptist rises just outside the gate of Detroit's historic Elmwood Cemetery, and by giving the church a vaulted doorway within a stylized peaked form, Birkerts evokes the cemetery's traditional gatehouse designed by Gordon Lloyd a century earlier.

Cathedral Church of St. Paul

4800 Woodward Avenue, Detroit

1911

Cram, Goodhue, and Ferguson

The Very Reverend Samuel S. Marquis, the first dean of the Cathedral Church of St. Paul, noted that this seat of the Episcopal Church in Detroit stood on one of the city's busiest thoroughfares, a symbol of the spiritual in the midst of all that is material, and a reminder of the invisible and eternal surrounded by the visible and temporal. Ralph Adams Cram, one of America's leading church architects, gave form to this high ideal in this elegant interpretation of the English Gothic Revival. The interior features a wealth of beautiful detail, including a tile floor designed by Mary Chase Perry Stratton, the founder of Pewabic Pottery. Interestingly, a square tower designed to rise over the crossing of the nave and the transepts has yet to be built.

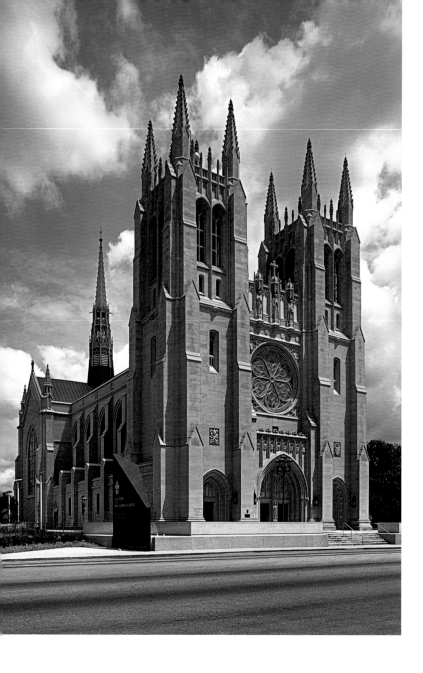

Cathedral of the Most Blessed Sacrament

9844 Woodward Avenue, Detroit

1915 with later additions

Henry A. Walsh, George Diehl

What started as a simple parish church proved so fine that the Roman Catholic Archdiocese transferred its seat of governance here in the 1930s. Yet the church structure wasn't completed until 1951 when the firm Diehl and Diehl completed the towers and renovated the interior to provide more space. In the 1990s, architect Gunnar Birkerts oversaw a modern updating. The church stands today as one of the city's most impressive Neo-Gothic structures with a wealth of beautiful detail.

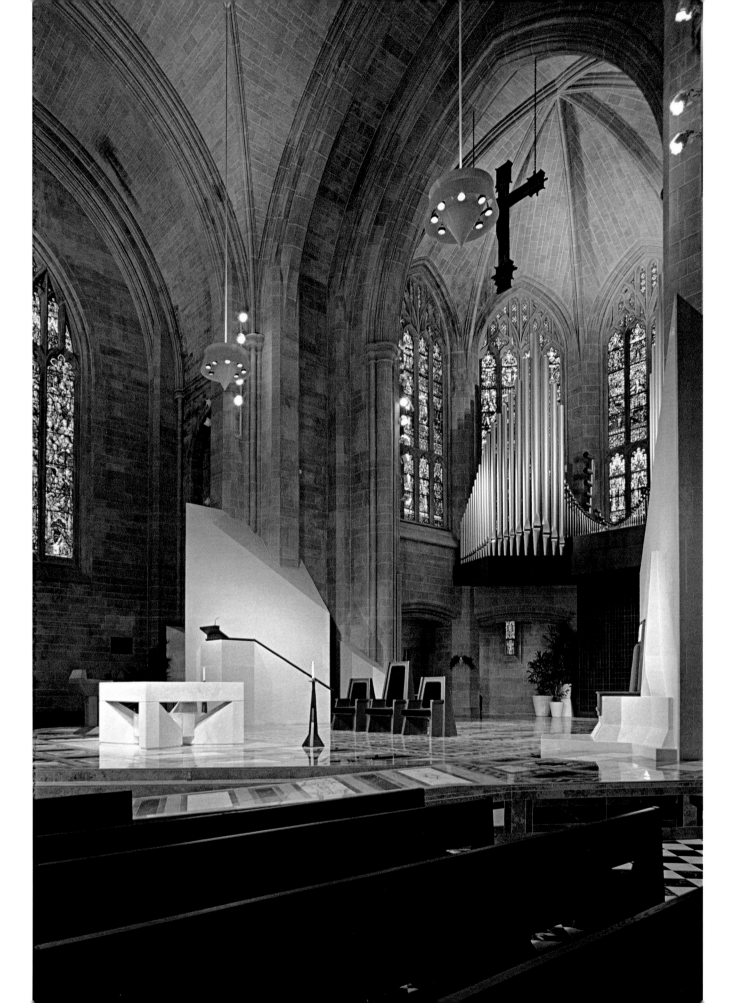

St. Mary Catholic Church

St. Antoine at Monroe, Detroit

1885

Peter Dederichs

A twin-spire church is always visually arresting, seldom more so than in this exuberant composition in what is now Detroit's Greektown district. St. Mary's remains one of Detroit's oldest active parishes, founded in the 1830s to serve the city's German-speaking Catholics. Completed in 1885, this current church building shows the hallmarks of the High Victorian sensibility, with its effusive blend of influences and detail. Yet designer Peter Dederichs worked so skillfully that everything came together in a harmonious creation. Though the church stands today in odd juxtaposition with Greektown Casino, it remains one of Detroit's architectural essentials.

Saint Florian Church

2626 Poland, Hamtramck

1928

Cram and Ferguson

Beyond their spiritual importance, parish churches in early 20th century Detroit often stood for the civic and ethnic pride of their communities. Detroit's Polish immigrant population swelled in the early '20s in response to jobs at local auto plants, and tens of thousands of these working-class Poles spilled over into Hamtramck, where they built Saint Florian. Noted Boston architect Ralph Adams Cram gave the church an English Gothic beauty, but his work was by no means strictly medieval. In the broad smooth planes, abstract massing, deeply punched opening and floating rose window, some observers see hints of the Post-Modernism of a much later day. Korab's photo perfectly sites Saint Florian's in its working class neighborhood, towering above but serving the needs of its parishioners.

7   BUILDINGS WE WORK IN

D.H. Day Farm

Near Glen Haven, Leelanau County

1880s and 1890s

Unknown designer

Some buildings blend so naturally with their surroundings that they seem to be of the earth rather than on it. So it is with the D.H. Day Farmstead, established more than a century ago by its namesake. Just farm buildings? Hardly. Look closer and notice the incredibly fine detailing. The massive dairy barn and silos are capped by very fine bell-shaped roofs; there is the subtle curve of the peak of the barn roof; and the eaves flare out just enough to assist with rain runoff. Both visually and functionally a winner, this is architecture without pretense, a beautiful illustration of how we shape our buildings and then they shape us.

Fayette Iron Works

Fayette

Ca. 1870

Jackson Iron Company

Fayette's charcoal kilns, storage buildings and other purely functional structures prove that industry stripped to its essence can produce a beauty all its own. Unselfconsciously beautiful, the iron works evoke ancient Indian ruins or medieval castles. In historical fact, this town site once boasted one of the Upper Peninsula's most productive iron-smelting centers. It is located on the Garden Peninsula at Snail Shell Harbor. About 500 residents lived and worked here during the 1870s and '80s, but the town declined quickly after the Jackson Iron Company closed its smelting operation in 1891. In more recent years, the site has been located in the state's Fayette Historic State Park.

River Rouge Ford Plant

Miller Road, Dearborn
1917–28; later revisions
Albert Kahn

The Rouge became Henry Ford's ultimate expression of unified and efficient production. Begun in 1917 and first used to manufacture wartime ships, the Rouge by the 1930s employed more than 100,000 workers on 2,000 acres. As Ford envisioned, his "ore to assembly" system could take in raw materials, turn them into glass and steel, and roll out finished Model As at the other end. Ford employed architect Albert Kahn to design the complex, and Kahn, that lover of Renaissance architecture and fine music, infused Ford's plants with an artist's sensibility to light and openness. His design for the Glass Plant, with its column-free work areas and its heavily windowed upper reaches to assist with light and cooling, marked something new in industrial design, a marvel of style integrating with function.

General Motors Technical Center

*Mound Road between 12
and 13 Mile, Warren*

1956

Eero Saarinen

This monumental collection of buildings proved to be more than a home for General Motors' design and engineering labs. It also marked an astounding leap into the future of architecture. Under the inspired hand of Eero Saarinen, the team of notable designers all but reinvented many construction products and techniques. They used neoprene gaskets to hold in windows (as in a car) instead of caulk, and employed new roof trusses and wall panels that allowed vastly more open space within. Everywhere we see the ethic of engineering innovation expressed — in the two "floating" staircases designed by Kevin Roche, in the ceramic glazed bricks on the exterior, in the water ballet (designed by Alexander Calder) in the man-made lake, in the futuristic water tower, and in the design dome. Half a century on, Saarinen's gem still dazzles.

A sort of playground for creative adults, Herman Miller's Design Yard is where a company known the world around for its museum-quality chairs develops and tests new office furniture. Set in rural Michigan outside Holland, the design yard is meant to evoke one of the neighboring farmsteads, even if many of the buildings, like the bright red silos atop fieldstone bases, tweak the form more than a little. Inside past the lobby, it's all fun mixed with work: Don't be surprised to see prototypes of the latest chair, cubicle, or desk coming in for intense if good-natured debate.

Herman Miller Design Yard

375 West 48th Street, Holland

1989

Meyer, Scherer and Rockcastle

John D. Dingell VA Hospital and Medical Center

4646 John R, Detroit

1996

Smith, Hinchman & Grylls

This enormous veterans hospital posed a challenge to designers — how to break down the scale so it didn't look like some monstrous Soviet office block? The solution proved surprisingly adept: An ingenious use of color to indicate various functions, and an overall massing distinguished by curved bays, partial cornices, and other architectural motifs, all enlivened by a bright enameled "wet" look. The eye tends to focus on individual forms rather than on the massive whole. Inside, a light-filled courtyard is enriched by a strikingly original glass-block chapel. The hospital was one of the final buildings created by the veteran Smith, Hinchman & Grylls under that name; it soon morphed into its new identity as SmithGroup.

Cadillac Place

3044 West Grand Boulevard, Detroit

1922

Albert Kahn

Perhaps nothing revealed Detroit's growing automotive might as this monumental structure built to house General Motors headquarters. Under the sure hand of Albert Kahn, the elements of early skyscraper design, including a Renaissance arcade at the street, unornamented "shaft" and Corinthian colonnade at the top, were given a vigorous new application. The second-largest office building in the world at its creation, the structure featured four identical cross-wings branching off from the central spine so that all of the individual offices could enjoy sunlight and fresh air. After GM moved its headquarters to the Renaissance Center in the 1990s, the State of Michigan moved into the impressively renovated landmark.

Durant-Dort Carriage Company

315 West Water Street, Flint

1895

Owners William Durant and J. Dallas Dort

From these humble beginnings sprang the mighty General Motors Corp. Two partners, William Durant and J. Dallas Dort, teamed up in the mid-1890s to produce horse-drawn vehicles, switching in time to Buick cars. The site is now part of Flint's historic Carriage Town district. Their building initially had two stories; they enlarged it after a few years by adding the upper portion. The red-brick, hipped-roof structure with the dormer windows projecting from the roof looks decidedly residential; compare it with General Motors' current world headquarters, the gleaming 73-story Renaissance Center in Detroit.

Kresge Foundation Headquarters

3215 West Big Beaver Road, Troy

1852; 2006

Washington Stanley; Valerio Dewalt Train

The classic Michigan farmstead came first, built when today's bustling Big Beaver corridor was gentle farmland. The beautiful Greek Revival house, barn, and other buildings remained in agricultural use until the 1960s when, threatened by encroaching development, they were purchased by the non-profit Kresge Foundation for use as offices. In 2006, a stunningly modern yet entirely sympathetic addition integrated seamlessly with the original buildings. Kresge Foundation, a leader in encouraging "green" design, employed dozens of environmentally sensitive initiatives in its new building. Thus the old and new tell a story of earth-friendly design carried through the generations.

Fisher Building

3011 West Grand Boulevard, Detroit

1929

Albert Kahn

Perhaps no Michigan clients ever splurged like the Fisher brothers when they asked Albert Kahn to design the world's finest office building. Did he deliver! The interior of this Detroit landmark features a three-story vaulted arcade finished with 40 different marbles, solid bronze trim, and multiple other ornaments. The dramatic silhouette of the tower owes much to both Romanesque precedents and Art Deco imagery and is probably the finest in the city. Some lament that the Fisher brothers' full program for two other towers, one at least twice as high as this building, did not survive the Depression. But the loss leaves the sole Fisher Building as a unique masterpiece. Voted the "Building of the Century" by the members of AIA Detroit.

Guardian Building

500 Griswold Street, Detroit

1929

Smith, Hinchman & Grylls

By any measure, the Guardian Building dazzles. Wirt Rowland of SH&G, fresh from his triumph at the nearby Penobscot Building, ventured into new terrain with this Art Deco masterpiece, blending fine brickwork, glazed tile, terra cotta, and even painted fabric to achieve new combinations of form, texture, and color. The multiple mosaics and Pewabic tiles, the huge vaulted main banking floor, and the lively murals all attest to the ebullience of the 1920s and Rowland's vision. Recently restored by SH&G's successor firm SmithGroup, which makes its Detroit office here, and even more recently purchased by Wayne County to house government offices, the Guardian remains a Michigan treasure.

Penobscot Building

645 Griswold Street, Detroit

1928

Smith, Hinchman & Grylls

With its tapering setbacks and its dramatic height, this 47-story skyscraper arose during Detroit's architecturally golden 1920s and remained the city's tallest building until the Renaissance Center a half-century later. Crafted by the famous Wirt Rowland of SH&G, the Penobscot marked a dramatic forward shift in tall-building design in Detroit. After this, no longer could classical wedding-cake ornament define a skyscraper; slender massing and vertical reach dominated from here on. Today, nighttime exterior lighting of the upper floors creates an added visual impact. And with shops on three levels and busy foot traffic, the Penobscot remains as lively at street level as it does on the skyline.

Renaissance Center

East Jefferson at Brush, Detroit

1977

John Portman

Detroit's postcard image, the Renaissance Center is all gleaming dark glass, as impersonal perhaps as the tinted windows of a rich man's limousine, yet a powerful expression of a city's pride all the same. The four 39-story octagonal office towers surrounding the 73-story hotel cylinder are probably more abstract than related directly to its site. And the interior labyrinth has long confused even those familiar with it. After General Motors bought the building for its world headquarters in the mid-1990s, it hired Skidmore, Owings & Merrill to do some major editing of Portman's design. SOM inserted a suspended circulation ring in the interior that aids navigation considerably; the creation of the light-filled Wintergarden and a new riverside plaza helped even more. With the Ren Cen's weaknesses thus diminished, its strengths emerge even more clearly.

Octagon Barn Purdy Farm

Ritchie Road near Gagetown

1924

James Purdy, John and George Munro

Farmer James Purdy built his barn to raise Black Angus cattle, and underlying the unusual design is an efficient system for feeding and caring for livestock. Inside the huge timber-framed structure, an overhead tram helped with the loading and unloading of hay. Unusual for this type of building, the two-stage roof is pierced with multiple windows to allow in light. Now a Michigan historic site, the building that locals call the Round Barn is home to numerous craft shows, school outings, live music, and multiple demonstrations of old-time farm operations.

David Stott Building

1150 Griswold Street, Detroit

1929

Donaldson and Meier

Like no other building in Detroit, this slim shaft of orange-tan brick captured the ideal of architect Eliel Saarinen's famed (but never built) entry in the Chicago Tribune Tower competition. Mostly lacking in historical ornament, the David Stott demonstrated that a skyscraper drew its power from its elemental massing and dramatic verticals. After this and a few other towers with clean, sharp lines in the 1920s, most architects stopped decorating their skyscrapers with historical froufrou — at least, that is, until the advent of the post-Modernists five decades later.

Ford Motor Co. World Headquarters

American Road near Michigan Avenue, Dearborn

1956

Skidmore, Owings & Merrill

Even after a half century, the headquarters of Ford Motor Co. looks refreshingly crisp and new. Architects at Skidmore, Owings & Merrill had already done much to create the modern glass-walled office building in the United States; here they advanced the form in important ways. To free up space on the interior, support columns were kept to the outside, while escalators helped with interior navigation of the enormous floor plates. Popularly known as the Glass House, the building is set far back from the busy roadways, allowing it to be admired from all sides like a model car on display.

One Woodward

1 Woodward Avenue, Detroit
(below, far left)
1963
Minoru Yamasaki with
Smith, Hinchman & Grylls

The great Minoru Yamasaki softened the International Style by draping a delicate vertical grillwork around this 32-story skyscraper. An elegant 30-foot high glass-enclosed lobby added further refinement, as did the outdoor reflecting pool with a sculpture by Giacomo Manzu. The overall effect is of lightness and grace. Many see this as a smaller version of Yamasaki's World Trade Center towers built later in New York City. Most agree Yama achieved considerably more artistic success in Detroit with the idea than he did in Gotham.

Stroh River Place

Joseph Campau at the Detroit River, Detroit
1891–1930; adaptive reuse 1980s
Multiple architects

Built in stages by the pharmaceutical company
Parke-Davis, this complex of two dozen or so
buildings on the Detroit River was an early pro-
totype of today's corporate campus. Beginning
in the 1980s, the Stroh brewing family took over
the then-empty structures and converted them
into retail, dining, office space, and residential
lofts. Rare among Detroit's waterfront projects
in the '80s, Stroh River Place did not barricade
itself behind security fences; its embrace of urban
vitality looks wiser with each passing year. Numerous significant architects have contributed over
the decades either to the original complex or the
remake, including such notables as Albert Kahn,
Donaldson and Meier, and James Stewart Polshek.

People's State Bank

151 West Fort Street, Detroit

1900

McKim, Mead and White

This Beaux-Arts classicism building has hosted so many different businesses over the years that it deserves some sort of prize. It began as a bank — the only building in Detroit (other than a mausoleum) designed by the famed Stanford White and his partners. Much later it became part of an office supply chain, then a clothing store, and still later a training school for computer workers. It even got tricked out as a temporary nightclub during Super Bowl XL in 2006. Through it all, the elegance of the original design continued to shine through. A little-known fact is that McKim, Mead and White created only the front half of the building; in 1914, a sympathetic addition by Donaldson and Meier extended it down to Congress.

Traverse City State Hospital

Division and Eleventh, Traverse City

1885

Gordon W. Lloyd

In the later years of the 19th century, the best psychiatric minds believed the "insane" could be cured in clean, efficient, well-designed facilities like this. The state hired prestigious Detroit architect Gordon W. Lloyd to create the plan here, and the Victorian-Italianate building was sited amid more than 300 acres of rolling, wooded terrain. Administrative offices were housed in the central portion while men's and women's wings spread out to either side. Various support buildings were added later. The state closed the asylum in 1989 as part of the move toward deinstitutionalizing the mentally ill. In recent years, the adaptively reused site has hosted a marketplace, day care, arts center, and other uses.

Quincy Mining Co. Historic District

Hancock vicinity

1850s–1920

Quincy Copper Mining Company

The Quincy Copper Mining Company, one of some 400 mining operations along the Keweenaw Peninsula at the height of Michigan's late 19th-and-early 20th-century copper boom, was known as Old Reliable for its more than half-century of steady output. Structures like the towering headframe of Mine Shaft No. 2, which dates to the early 1900s and is one of the few survivors of the era, remind us today of this hugely important industry. Demand was so great that the mine drew workers from the copper mines of Cornwall, England. Technologically advanced, the operation could lift several tons of copper from more than a mile deep in the earth in just two minutes or so.

Pewabic Pottery

10125 East Jefferson, Detroit

1907

Stratton and Baldwin

After Mary Chase Perry founded her Pewabic Pottery Company in 1903 (naming it after a copper mine in her native Upper Peninsula), she asked her friend (and later husband) William Stratton to design its new center. Inspired by the English Arts & Crafts movement, Stratton crafted a building that blended elements of Tudor and English domestic revival to perfectly reflect the craftsman aesthetic. Notice the chimneys made of different materials, the overhanging eaves, the varied window types, and the mix of materials on the exterior — all motifs of the Arts & Crafts style. From this humble setting, the work of Pewabic Pottery has enriched houses, churches, and numerous other buildings near and far.

Marquette County Savings Bank

125 West Washington Street, Marquette

1892

Barber and Barber

The thriving mining community of Marquette deserved and got a modern bank and office tower in the early 1890s. The building has stood as a local landmark ever since. Five stories in front rising to the seven-story clock tower on one corner, the building seems taller than it is, as the semi-circular bays rising above the narrower base, and of course the clock tower, dramatize the vertical. Here, generations of Yoopers kept their savings and enjoyed views sloping down toward mighty Lake Superior.

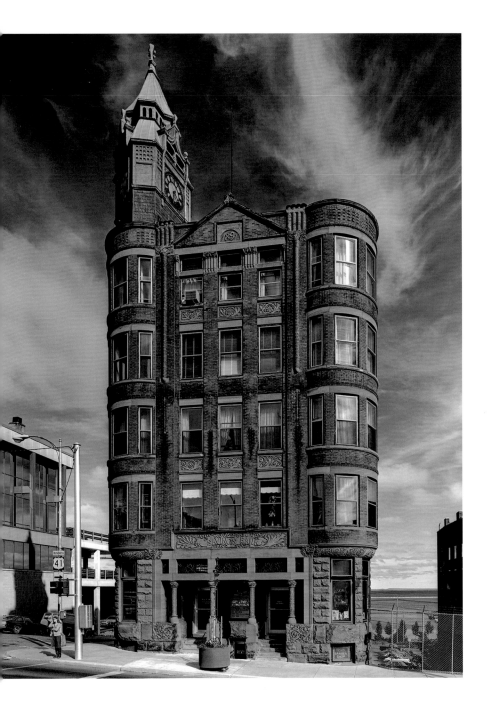

Domino's Farms

M-14 and US-23, Ann Arbor

1985

Gunnar Birkerts

Tom Monaghan, the founder of Domino's Pizza, has pursued many passions in his life, among them his enthusiasm for Frank Lloyd Wright's work. So when architect Gunnar Birkerts suggested a modern take on Wright's Prairie Style for Domino's corporate headquarters, Monaghan grabbed the chance. They built from the ends in, leaving a gap that wasn't filled until 2005, but today the low-slung, four-story building runs more than half a mile. The copper roof is said to be the longest in the United States and possibly in the world. Not the least of the charms is that Monaghan surrounded it with pastures, cultivated farmland, and a wildlife habitat. Don't be surprised to see bison roaming the grounds as you motor past on M-14.

Detroit Cornice and Slate Co.

733 St. Antoine, Detroit
1897; renovation and addition 1999
Harry J. Rill;
William Kessler and Associates

The original building here sported one of Detroit's most effusive façades. The Beaux-Arts confection was not, despite its look, carved stone. Rather, Detroit Cornice and Slate made architectural ornament from pressed and hand-hammered steel that was then (as we see here) painted to resemble a more expensive limestone or marble. In the 1990s, the *Metro Times* newspaper, by then a tenant, engaged Kessler and Associates to renovate and expand the space for office use. The sleekly modern north façade provides both a sharp contrast and a respectful nod to the original.

One Detroit Center

500 Woodward Avenue, Detroit

1992

Johnson Burgee Architects

One of Detroit's few examples of the Post-Modern architectural movement that swept (some say defaced) numerous cities in the 1980s and '90s, One Detroit Center is also notable as the city's only offering from the legendary Philip Johnson and his partner John Burgee. The spiky top could be interpreted as Flemish Gothic or something out of a Batman movie. Otherwise the tower is mainstream commercial architecture enriched by generous use of granites and marbles inside and out. A dominant image on the skyline, One Detroit Center provided a shot of adrenaline downtown during the long drought between the Renaissance Center in the 1970s and the rebuilding that has enlivened downtown in the first decade of the new century.

Saginaw Water Works

522 Ezra Rust Drive, Saginaw

1929

Victor Andre Matteson

Perhaps citizens once held government in greater esteem than they do now. That would explain how even a lowly water treatment plant could get such a lofty architectural garb. Modeled after English Gothic university towns (think Oxford and Cambridge), the water works benefits from a good site, too, nestled within Ezra Rust Park near a small lake. In Korab's photo, it rises like country manor house of yore, screened by trees, reflected in the waters of the lake, a vision of tranquility and order.

Buhl Building

535 Griswold Street, Detroit (below, foreground)

1925

Smith, Hinchman & Grylls

You can almost see Wirt Rowland, the talented designer for SH&G, struggling to shape a modern skyscraper out of classical clay. Among other innovations, he left off the traditional cornice to achieve a more vertical silhouette. And the cross-plan, with four wings emerging from a central core, was a new way to bring light and air to the interior of a tall building. Within a few short years, Rowland would add two more brilliant designs to downtown's skyline, the Penobscot and the Guardian. But those masterpieces may not have been possible had Rowland not taken the first tentative steps here at the Buhl. Even today, three-quarters of a century later, the Buhl and its many tenants help anchor the downtown financial district.

Nickels Arcade

326–330 South State Street, Ann Arbor

1918

Herman Pipp

Long before the suburban mall became the American way to shop, local businessman Tom Nickels figured out a way to extend Ann Arbor's State Street commercial strip facing the University of Michigan campus. The 265-foot skylighted walkway connecting State and Maynard is lined with first-floor shops and upper level offices. Architect Herman Pipp crafted a distinguished look of classical forms melded with Art Deco imagery. Arcades weren't exactly a new idea; earlier examples included the Galleria Vittorio Emanuele II in Milan, Italy, or, closer to home, the Market Arcade in Buffalo, N.Y. But Nickels and Pipp perfectly fitted the idea to the Ann Arbor streetscape.

Detroit Receiving Hospital

4201 St. Antoine, Detroit

1980

William Kessler and Associates;

Zeidler Partnership; Giffels Associates

William Kessler's Detroit Receiving Hospital intro-
duced something new into the idea of a hospital
even beyond the silvery, high-tech look. The various buildings are arranged in cross-like forms with
interconnected modules around 48-foot-square light
wells, creating a new openness where older hospitals
had offered cramped corridors. The trademark skin
consists of aluminum panels, ribbon windows, and
enameled splashes of color. The composition as a
whole can be read as symbolic of modern medical
marvels. A work of art by itself, the hospital displays
an extensive collection of paintings and sculpture
that, in their own way, contribute to the healing arts.

8 BUILDINGS WE LIVE IN

Honolulu House

107 North Kalamazoo Avenue, Marshall
1860
Attributed to William L. Buck

The town of Marshall in south-central Michigan has earned fame for its notable 19th century architecture, and the Honolulu House ranks among its best. Judge Abner Pratt served as U.S. Consul to the Sandwich (Hawaiian) Islands in the late 1850s, and upon his return he built this house to remind him of his Pacific sojourn. The home is said to resemble his official residence in Honolulu; besides the Polynesian influences, it also shows elements of Italianate and Gothic Revival. Like many of our greatest buildings in Michigan, this was threatened with demolition (for a gas station, no less!) but Marshall benefactor Harold Brooks bought the house in 1951 to protect it. Today it serves as home to the Marshall Historical Society, and as the focal point of Marshall's National Historic Landmark District.

Miners Houses

Along Red Jacket Road, Calumet

1870–1910

Calumet and Hecla Mining Company

Copper mining was to 19th century Michigan what automotive manufacturing was in the 20th century, and no company town thrived during that earlier era like Calumet in the far northwestern Upper Peninsula. The C&H company built some 1,200 homes for its workers, not to mention schools, a hospital, a library, and much more. Many of the houses were two-and-a-half stories and shingle-sided, built on rock formations made of mine debris. There was, of course, a pecking order to these structures, with the more elaborate built for the professional class and the simpler variety for the miners themselves. As the business of extracting copper from the earth waned, many of the homes were bought by private owners for their use. Today Calumet is a national historic landmark where the story of the miners and their life is told with pride.

Fitch House

310 North Kalamazoo Avenue, Marshall

Ca. 1840

Unknown architect

One of Michigan's oldest surviving buildings and a prominent example of Greek Revival architecture. Over its life it has housed some of Marshall's most notable citizens, beginning with Jabez Fitch, the local merchant who built it for himself in the style popular then among the upwardly striving. In the 20th century, Harold C. Brooks, Marshall's pioneering preservationist, bought the house for his own use. Noted landscape architect Jens Jensen, mentioned elsewhere in this book for his work on both the Henry and Edsel Ford estates, designed the grounds in 1921.

Alden B. Dow Home and Studio

315 Post Street, Midland

1934–41

Alden B. Dow

Dow, an heir to the chemical fortune, was in his late 20s when he apprenticed with Frank Lloyd Wright in 1933, and soon afterward he built his studio in his hometown and went on to add his residence. Many see Wright's influences in the horizontal lines and overhanging eaves, but the home and studio really belong to Dow's own genius. The complex asymmetrical forms take full advantage of the lush vegetation and water. Dow created marvelous touches throughout, like the room set a full 18 inches below the level of the pond. In a trademark feature, one-foot-square concrete blocks seem to wander off the house into the water in ways entirely organic and natural. Beautifully maintained as a museum, it ranks among Michigan's very best of the best.

Goetsch-Winckler House

2410 Hulett Road, Okemos

1939

Frank Lloyd Wright

Even at his most successful, Frank Lloyd Wright never stopped trying to build affordable houses for people of modest means. A fine example is the home he designed for Alma Goetsch and Kathrine Winckler, two teachers in the art department of Michigan State University. To save them money, Wright eliminated the basement in favor of a slab and used a carport instead of a garage; the kitchen is partially incorporated into the living space in the mode of many modern apartments. Yet for all the economies employed, Wright still fitted the home into its natural setting and imbued it with his trademark sense of being of the earth rather than imposed on it. To the owners' friends viewing this revolutionary home in 1940-era Michigan, the impact must have been little short of astonishing.

Amariah T. Prouty House

302 Elm Street, Kalamazoo

1852

Unknown designer

The Prouty House in Kalamazoo ranks high among the state's best examples of Gothic-inspired cottages. Warmed by the sun in Korab's photo, the house displays the elaborate scrollwork of the roof gable, the medieval-style bay window known as an oriel, and the subtle Tudor arches of the veranda. Later generations of architects might scorn such historical references, but the home is a beauty and a survivor of a bygone time.

Richardi House

402 North Bridge Street, Bellaire

1895

Henry Richardi

Of all the picturesque Queen Anne-style homes in Michigan, none is finer than this masterpiece in northern Michigan not far from Torch Lake. Henry Richardi was a businessman who owned the Bellaire Wooden Ware Company in town, and some of the German woodworkers he employed in his factory helped ensure the finest craftsmanship in his home. The delightfully complex series of gables, bays, overhangs, and tower are held together by superb detail work. It was so good it graced the cover of Kathryn Bishop Eckert's landmark book *Buildings of Michigan*. Today the home operates as a highly rated B&B known as the Grand Victorian.

Dwarf or Mushroom Houses

Bounded by Park, Grant, and Clinton streets, Charlevoix

Mid-20th century

Earl A. Young

Also known locally as "Hansel and Gretel" homes, these extremely picturesque houses were designed to appeal to the romantic at heart. Earl A. Young, a self-trained real estate developer, crafted these fairy-tale dwellings out of boulders left behind by glaciers, timber from shipwrecks, local limestone, and whatever else struck his fancy. Over a span of 50 years, Young bought back ideas from his visits to English cottages and built from memory without any formal plans, specializing in undulating wood-shingle roofs and large fireplaces. Some of the houses are only 800 square feet and sized for Young's 5'4" height. Owning one comes complete with tourists stopping to take photos almost daily.

William and Mary Palmer House

227 Orchard Hills Drive, Ann Arbor

1952

Frank Lloyd Wright

Frank Lloyd Wright loved to gently cascade a home down a slope, and the house he designed very late in his career for the Palmer family is among the best of the type. Built of cypress, sand-molded brick, and fired blocks, the design included perforated brick walls to allow natural light to enhance the interior. Wright scholar Grant Hildebrand has noted that the Palmers, unlike many owners of a Wright home, lived in the house year-round for most of their lives. Children and grandchildren were married on its terrace, and friends were invited to stay. "They didn't use it as a museum," Hildebrand has said. "They lived there. Mary once asked me, 'Is it wrong to love a house so much?'"

Meyer May House

450 Madison Avenue SE, Grand Rapids

1909

Frank Lloyd Wright

This was Frank Lloyd Wright's first major commission in Michigan, and it remains an outstanding example of his Prairie style. Part of the Heritage Hill district overlooking downtown Grand Rapids, the house features all of Wright's signature motifs, from the shallow hipped roof to the broad overhangs and the skillful use of terraces and gardens to intermingle indoors and out. In the 1980s, the Steelcase furniture company acquired the house and undertook one of the most precise and complete restorations of a Wright home anywhere. Today, open for tours, it continues to inspire.

Lafayette Park

Bounded by Lafayette, Rivard, Orleans and Antietam, Detroit

1956–63

Ludwig Mies van der Rohe and Ludwig Hilberseimer

Perhaps unique among '50s-era urban development schemes, Lafayette Park proved the success that its creators hoped for and remains an urban oasis today. This was no doubt due in large part to the wisdom of Chicago developers who hired the best in the business. Working with landscape architect Alfred Caldwell, master planner Ludwig Hilberseimer mapped out the 78-acre cluster of residential components grouped around a central park; and architect Ludwig Mies van der Rohe crafted a series of high-rise and low-rise structures that emphasized privacy and serenity in the midst of the bustling city. Subtly enriching details enlivened the district, like putting the parking lots slightly below grade level so residents look out their windows to see landscaping and fine architecture, rather than cars. The maturing landscape over the years has only added to the park-like feel.

Douglas House

3490 Lake Shore Drive, north of Harbor Springs

1973

Richard Meier

The best modernist houses in Michigan tend to cluster in the Arts & Crafts school of Frank Lloyd Wright, Eliel and Eero Saarinen, and Alden B. Dow. Michigan boasts fewer of the purely geometric International style, and ever fewer of the quality of this early Richard Meier composition. Set on a sloping hillside overlooking Lake Michigan, the home offers a sharp contrast both to other vacation homes nearby and to the natural setting. Meier himself wrote that so steep was the slope that the house appeared to have been dropped into the site, "a machine-crafted object that has landed in a natural world, setting up a dramatic dialogue between the whiteness of the house and the primary blues and greens of the water, trees, and sky."

Charles Lang Freer House

71 East Ferry, Detroit

1890

Wilson Eyre, Jr.

Charles Lang Freer made his fortune manufacturing railroad cars, but he's remembered chiefly for his art collection, today housed in Washington, D.C.'s Freer Gallery of Art. Yet his home in Detroit remains in some ways his most notable effort. Foregoing the Gilded Age palaces favored by his contemporaries, Freer chose the quieter pleasures of a Shingle-style home. The beautifully textured shingled upper portion rises above a stone first floor, and the dominant roof with its overhanging eaves ties the composition together. The famous Peacock Room, now in Washington, was earlier housed here. As Detroit scholar Dr. Thomas W. Brunk writes, "His home, like many of the contemporary American paintings Freer collected, was not created for public exhibition; rather this home reflected his own cultivated taste and discreet collecting habits." Today it serves as home to the Merrill Palmer Skillman Institute, concerned with childhood development.

Amberg Cottage

West Bluff, Mackinac Island

1886, remodeled 1892

Asbury W. Buckley

Running just west of the Grand Hotel on Mackinac Island, West Bluff features a row of cottages that offer sweeping vistas of the Straits of Mackinac and a glimpse of summertime life during the Gilded Age. The Amberg Cottage is a large Queen Anne style house with picturesque towers, porches, and roof shingles. The rounded and octagonal corner towers and the many windows were designed with views of the water in mind. The white paint, so typical of West Bluff cottages, enhances the impression of easy, gracious living.

Andrus House

57500 Van Dyke Road, Washington Township

1860

David Stewart

In mid-19th century America, octagon or eight-sided houses enjoyed a flair due to their supposed economies of space planning and heating and cooling. The Andrus House ranks among Michigan's finest surviving examples. The most dramatic feature is the circular staircase that rises up through the middle of the house. Loren Andrus built this in 1860, using bricks fired on his farm from the local clay, and having his brother-in-law and local builder David Stewart design and construct it for him. Beginning in the 1930s, the house did duty as a restaurant, then an agricultural training center, and later a dormitory for farm students. Barely escaping the wrecking ball, it was purchased in 1986 by a non-profit group known today as Friends of the Octagon House, which, continually restoring it, operates the house as a museum and education center.

Gardner House (The Maples)

511 Green Street, Dowagiac

1897

William K. Johnston

Michigan has hosted many important industries beyond the automotive field. This picturesque home in the state's far southwestern corner got built thanks to money from the state's once-thriving stove manufacturing business. Archie B. Gardner served as the Round Oak Stove Co.'s treasurer when he built this sturdy, beautifully detailed house, and it became a local landmark (even more so after Gardner bought the first car to arrive in Dowagiac in 1899). Known as The Maples, the home is faced with massive boulders and trimmed with local sandstone; the dramatically composed roof is covered in red tiles. Korab's photo, taken at a time of year when trees were bare and grass brown, perfectly captures the austere beauty.

Hackley House

484 West Webster Avenue, Muskegon

1889

David S. Hopkins

Millionaire lumber baron Charles Hackley, who gifted a library seen elsewhere in this book to Muskegon, built this sumptuous home for himself and his wife. The style is Queen Anne, a picturesque blending of asymmetrical massing, polychromatic exteriors, and a wealth of gables, chimneys, porches, and bays. The woodcarvings alone are among the best residential work anywhere in the state, depicting human faces, dragons, lions, and flowers. The leaded glass windows and ceramic tile fireplace installations are also exceptional. The Muskegon County Museum has restored the house and operates it today, offering its many visitors a glimpse of life during Michigan's Gilded Age.

Meadow Brook Hall

Oakland University Campus, Rochester

1929

William Kapp of Smith, Hinchman & Grylls

When Matilda Dodge, widow of auto pioneer John Dodge, honeymooned in Great Britain with her second husband, lumber broker Alfred Wilson, the couple visited the ancient manor houses of England and later obtained precise drawings of them. Their resulting house in the then-rural landscape of Oakland County was completed in 1929, a 110-room, 88,000-square-foot mansion in the Tudor Revival style with some of the finest wood carvings, brickwork, interior decorations, and gardens anywhere. Ironically, the couple for some periods lived elsewhere on the estate when the hall itself proved too expensive and impractical to staff and heat. The home is now owned by Oakland University, which offers tours and uses it as a conference center. Meadow Brook Hall stands as one of America's castles, a beautifully preserved example of the use to which great wealth was once put.

Cudahy Cottage

West Bluff, Mackinac Island

1888

Unknown designer

Chicago meatpacker John Cudahy was among the wealthy vacationers who built summer homes for themselves on West Bluff, and a glance at this magnificent home hints at the privileges that great fortunes bestowed. The style is a blend of the Queen Anne and the Shingle, a picturesque composition of stone foundation, many towers, porches, and bays, and elaborately shingled exterior. If strolling or biking on West Bluff, don't be shy about taking pictures or simply standing and staring for awhile, for the home represents the pinnacle of Michigan cottage architecture.

Henry Ford quickly outgrew his Highland Park setting, and the indus-
trialist moved to Dearborn, where he had amassed more than 2,000
acres. Henry and his wife, Clara, hired Marion Mahony Griffin, a former
student of Frank Lloyd Wright, who was with the Chicago architectural
firm of Von Holst & Fyfe, to design them a Prairie style house. But a trip
to Europe, where they saw and appreciated English manor homes, altered
their plans, as did a construction dispute with Von Holst & Fyfe. Hiring
William Van Tine to redo the plans, the Fords got a unique blend of the
baronial and the Prairie. The extensive grounds were sculpted by Jens
Jensen, who also did the work at the Edsel and Eleanor Ford Home. Today,
owned by the University of Michigan, Henry and Clara's Fair Lane serves
as a conference center and a memorial to what the Fords built.

Fair Lane (Henry Ford Estate)

4901 Evergreen Road, Dearborn

1915

William Van Tine, with Von Holst & Fyfe

DePree House

Division Street and Rich Avenue, Zeeland

1954

Charles Eames

One of Michigan's unique houses, from the hand of Charles Eames, the internationally famous furniture designer retained by Herman Miller Company. Eames crafted this modernistic house for Max DePree, son of the founder of Herman Miller and later the company president himself. In some ways it bears resemblance to Eames' famous Case Study #8 in California, a horizontal two-story house with a distinctly modular look. This version, though, is softer and warmer, and built by local craftsmen. The overall impression of tranquility is reinforced by the woodsy site.

Gregor Affleck House

1925 North Woodward Avenue, Bloomfield Hills

1941

Frank Lloyd Wright

This home came relatively late in Wright's long career, when the master was already in his 70s. By then, he could almost shake new buildings out of his sleeve, and the home he designed for the Affleck family shows an ease and assurance that are remarkable even today. L-shaped in plan, the house is arranged so that the bedroom wing fits at a right angle to the living room; the point of juncture is marked by a light well where a reflecting pool below and the sky above are both visible. The most prominent feature is a deck thrust into nature, reminiscent of Wright's masterpiece Fallingwater. Today the home is owned by Lawrence Technological University, a worthy caretaker. Visited by many students, scholars, and devoted fans each year, it is probably Wright's best-known creation in Michigan.

Hecker House

5510 Woodward Avenue, Detroit

1891

Louis Kamper

This ranks high among Michigan's rare but incredibly fine examples of French Chateau architecture. Col. Frank J. Hecker was a Union Army veteran and manufacturer (his friend and partner, Charles Lang Freer, built his own home right next door), and Hecker's sumptuous mansion with its 49 rooms and elegant marbles hints at what Detroit's Gilded Age must have been like. In later years, a piano sales company occupied the house; today it is home to a prominent law firm. In any guise, it remains one of the city's treasures. When he designed this, architect Louis Kamper was just emerging as the city's master of opulent historical styles; he went on to craft the famed Book-Cadillac Hotel in the 1920s, and died in 1953 as the Grand Old Man of Detroit architecture.

David Whitney, Jr. House

4421 Woodward Avenue, Detroit

1894

Gordon W. Lloyd

Michigan's epoch as a 19th century timber capital produced its share of millionaires, and lumber baron David Whitney, Jr. clearly was one who had the money to indulge his family's whims. Architect Gordon Lloyd, nearing the end of his long and distinguished career in Detroit, concocted a rather overcooked exterior based on Romanesque Revival motifs. The sumptuous interior is better, with a bevy of rooms that rank among the city's most ornate. Thanks to its conversion to use as an elegant restaurant, the house remains open to anyone for the cost of a meal, albeit a fairly expensive one. Worth a visit.

Village of Bay View

U.S. 31 just north of Petoskey

1875–1900

Multiple designers

It's hard to find a place that better captures the spirit of a Michigan summer "up north" than Bay View. Methodist in origin and still associated with the United Methodist Church, Bay View serves as an ecumenical, Chautauqua-type summer colony where music, education, and intellectual discussion mix easily with boating, tennis, and other recreational pursuits. Today Bay View is comprised of more than 440 cottages, most dating to the late 1800s, and over 30 public buildings. The community's collection of summer cottages ranks among the best in Michigan. To drive or bicycle through on a summer day is to be transported back in time.

Edsel and Eleanor Ford House

1100 Lake Shore Road, Grosse Pointe Shores

1927

Albert Kahn

A lot of Michigan's early auto barons built themselves mansions, yet few but Edsel and Eleanor Ford took the care, had the funds, or hired as skilled an architect as Albert Kahn. The result operates today as a museum; it remains a must-see on a tour of Detroit automotive and architectural history. Kahn and his clients were inspired by English Cotswold cottages, and the Fords visited England to see the originals first hand. Not incidentally, they purchased many interior details to be reinstalled in Grosse Pointe. English stonemasons and roofers were imported to ensure authenticity. The grounds, offering sweeping views of Lake St. Clair, were sculpted by noted landscape architect Jens Jensen. Not just a mere period copy, the home was a living space for a real family, and some rooms were made over in a streamlined Art Deco style as tastes changed.

Detroit offers many old, distinguished neighborhoods, but perhaps none has fared so well over the years as this east side district of broad lawns and notable architecture. Built mostly during the formative years of the city's automotive boom, the district features numerous examples of fine materials and workmanship; the range of styles includes Arts & Crafts, Federal, Tudor, Renaissance, and more. The creation of a feisty neighborhood association in 1937 signaled a willingness to fight encroaching blight and the subdivision of the homes into apartments. That fight continues today, one reason why few districts in the city have maintained their original elegance so well as Indian Village.

Indian Village

Burns, Iroquois, and Seminole between Jefferson and Mack, Detroit

1894–1925

Multiple architects

Walter Briggs III House

Harbor Springs

1974

William Kessler

Captured at sunset on a wintry day by Korab's lens, the Briggs House could be Michigan's ideal "up north" cottage. The generous use of windows allows natural light to pour in, and the house, while large, tucks itself so gently into the terrain that it seems a natural part of the landscape. The architects softened the somewhat abstract massing by covering most of the exterior surface with beautifully textured shingles.

Hannah House

305 Sixth Street, Traverse City

1891

William G. Robinson

Lumber baron Perry Hannah and his wife built this 40-room mansion in the Queen Anne style, but what really sets it apart is a lumberman's insistence on the most elaborate carvings and woodwork inside and out. Each interior room is paneled in a different type of wood, and the various fireplaces and the ceremonial staircase and balcony all attest to local pride in Michigan's forests. Since the 1930s, the house has operated as a funeral home. Recognizing the home's importance, the funeral home offers a virtual tour online at www.reynolds-jonkhoff.com.

Reynolds Jonkhoff
FUNERAL HOME

Parkwyn Village

Taliesin Drive, Kalamazoo

1947–49

Frank Lloyd Wright

Michigan is home to some of Frank Lloyd Wright's finer efforts to build modest houses for people of middle incomes. In the late 1940s, Wright mapped plans for Parkwyn Village as a cooperative community featuring more than 40 of his so-called Usonian Automatic houses, simple and affordable and close to nature; the buyers were to be young scientists at the Upjohn Company. Only four Wright houses were actually built at Parkwyn Village, but, as Korab's photo shows, they typify Wright's concern for homes that provide shelter, privacy, and a connection to the natural world. Wright, of course, tinkered for decades with plans for his ideal Broadacre City. In Parkwyn Village, we see a tiny piece of what he had in mind.

Herbert and Grace Dow House

1038 West Main Street, Midland

1899

Clark and Munger

It's easy to see where the great architect Alden B. Dow got his genes. His father, the founder of the Dow Chemical Co., and mother built this rambling house in 1899 and upgraded over the years in a way that made a deep impression on their son. The overall style married the Shingle with the newly popular Arts & Crafts movement. The entry foyer is exceptional for its woodwork. Not the least of the home's attractions is the way it blends with the gardens that Herbert created and that Alden expanded decades later. Today the house is open for tours by appointment and is part of the extensive Dow Gardens in Midland.

Beaubien House

553 East Jefferson Avenue, Detroit

1851; restoration 1980s

Unknown architect

This stately three-story townhouse was among many that lined Detroit's East Jefferson Avenue in the Civil War era and that gave the early city a sturdy elegance. One of the lone survivors of that time (many such homes were razed for parking lots a century later), it was carefully restored by the Michigan Chapter of the American Institute of Architects in the 1980s. Today it serves as home to the state and local chapters of AIA and the Michigan Architectural Foundation. Standing in the shadow of the towering Renaissance Center across the street, the house also serves as a gentle reminder of a bygone era.

William Kessler House

1013 Cadieux, Grosse Pointe Park

1959

Meathe, Kessler and Associates

Architect William Kessler was a Harvard-trained modernist who graced Michigan with many notable buildings, including Detroit Receiving Hospital. For his own home, he crafted this light-as-air ranch that manages to create a zone of privacy even along a busy suburban street. He achieved the effect in part by running a garden wall the width of the front façade, allowing the side facing the private yard in back to consist most of glass walls. Ethereal yet cozy, the home remains a gem half-a-century on.

David Mackenzie House

4735 Cass Avenue, Detroit

1895

Malcomson and Higginbotham

Scholar David Mackenzie built this home for himself in the Queen Anne style, and it shows many characteristics of the type, with picturesque massing, the elaborate conical-roofed tower, and a variety of exterior surface materials. Much later, Mackenzie went on to found Detroit Junior College, from which Wayne State University sprang. Today, Mackenzie's house represents one of Michigan's great preservation wins. It was slated for demolition in 1975 to make way for a sewer line, but two Wayne State classmates, Allen Wallace and Marilyn Florek, rallied like-minded people to convince the university to save it. Today it serves as the headquarters of Preservation Wayne, Detroit's leading non-profit advocate for historic architecture.

Stratton House

938 Three Mile Drive, Grosse Pointe Park

1927

William B. Stratton

Architect William B. Stratton designed many buildings in the Arts & Crafts mode, and his wife, Mary Chase Perry Stratton, won even greater fame as a ceramic artist and founder of Pewabic Pottery. When they moved to Grosse Pointe Park, they reused many of the materials from their older home in Detroit, including beams, doors, windows, tile, and furniture, all reflecting the Arts & Crafts code of unique workmanship. Stratton designed the home with a nod to the emerging modernist aesthetic, with unadorned exterior brick walls and a more abstract massing than in his design of the Pewabic Pottery building of 1907. Everywhere, though, we see a craftsman's eye for texture and material. Inside and out, a masterpiece.

Turkel House

2760 West Seven Mile Road, Detroit

1956

Frank Lloyd Wright

America's most famous architect designed many houses in Michigan but only one in the city of Detroit and that one very late in his career. The Turkel house fell into what Wright called his "Usonian Automatic" category, homes built with mostly inexpensive materials but infused with the openness and ceremony that he championed. Framed entirely by concrete blocks, the house is an L-shaped, 4,000-square-foot structure, unusual for the Usonian model in being two stories. Set in Detroit's upscale Palmer Woods district, it stands out as a bold experiment in an area filled with Tudor and other historical styles. No doubt Wright would have appreciated any discomfort he caused the neighbors.

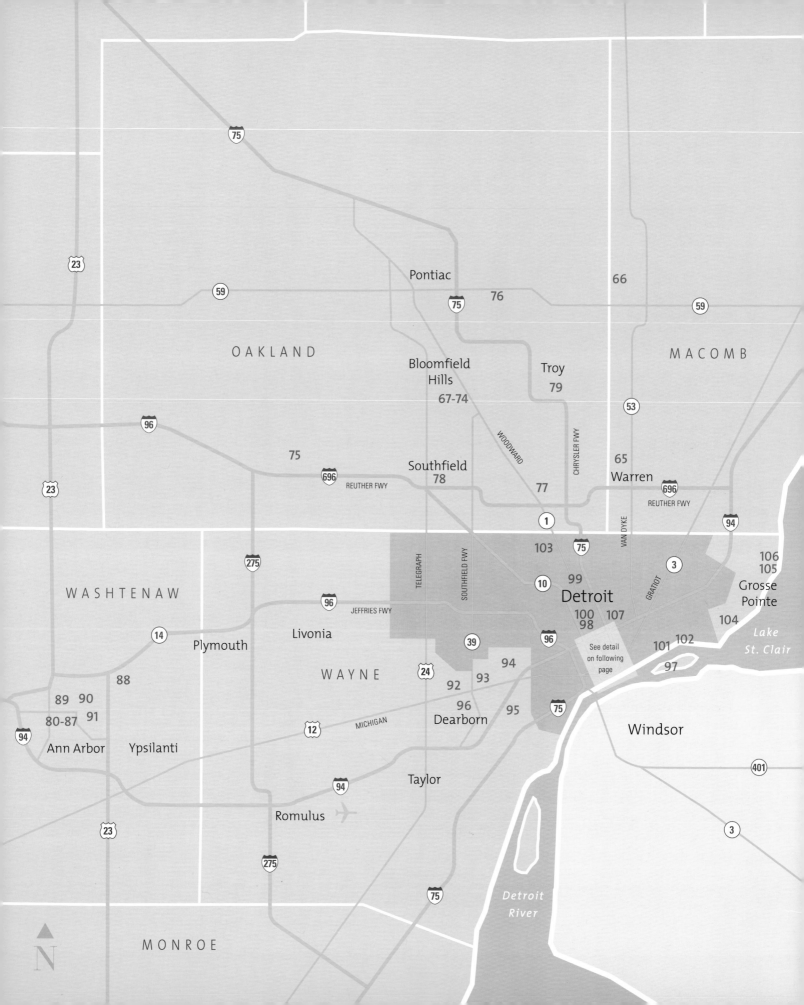

Index

Acknowledgments

The authors wish to thank the Michigan Architectural Foundation for making this book possible. Special thanks go to Carl Roehling, FAIA, president of the Foundation's Board of Directors, for his support and enthusiasm, and to Eric J. Hill, FAIA, for seeing the project through its formative stages. Thanks also to Mike Savitski and Adamo D'Aristotile of Savitski Design for their design of this book; to Christian Korab, who undertook the task of digitally mastering the images taken by his father over many decades; and to Sandra Knight Pogue, who as project manager kept the process moving forward. The authors also wish to thank Jane Hoehner and Kathryn Wildfong from Wayne State University Press for their help and advice. Finally, we thank our attentive copy editors Mary Hashman and Julie Truettner for their many thoughtful suggestions to improve the manuscript.

We thank the following individuals and firms, whose financial support
have helped make *Great Architecture of Michigan* possible:

Patrons

John W. Allegretti, FAIA

Ronald R. Campbell, AIA

Sue and Randy Case, AIA

Comerica Bank

Robert and Rae Dumke, Hon. AIA

Jeanne and Ralph Graham, Hon. Aff. AIAMI

Rainy Hamilton Jr., AIA, NOMA

Harley Ellis Devereaux Corporation

Janice and Jeffrey Hausman, AIA

Edie and Doug Kueffner, AIA

Diane and Phillip Lundwall, FAIA

Ben Maibach III

Michael A. Marshburn, AIA

Thomas R. and Denise L. Mathison

Cynthia Kozak Pozolo, AIA

Frank A. Ray, AIA

Barb and Carl Roehling, FAIA

Matthew Rossetti, AIA

Gary L. Skog, FAIA

J. Park Smith, AIA

Stephen Smith, AIA

A. Alfred Taubman

Leslie and Marion Tincknell and Family

Sue and Steve Whitney, FAIA

Donors

Bob and Jerri Carington

Dr. James Chaffers

Paul A. Corneliussen, AIA

Robert Warren Daverman, AIA

Carey M. Demas, AIA, NOMA

Pamela and Blake Elderkin, AIA

Nancy M. Finegood, Hon. Aff. AIAMI

Anthony A. Foust, AIA

Edward D. Francis, FAIA

Lynne Merrill-Francis

Juliana E. Garner, AIA

Eric J. Hill, FAIA

Herbert P. Jensen, AIA

Douglas Kelbaugh, FAIA and Kathleen Nolan

Janet L. Kreger, Hon. Aff. AIAMI

Daniel Launstein, AIA

Morris A. Lifshay, AIA, NCARB, AICP, RCO

Gail D. McClure

Cathy and Mike Mosley, AIA

Nelson Breech Nave, AIA

Arthur E. Nelson, AIA

Leo G. Shea, FAIA

Mr. and Mrs. Albert J. Vegter, AIA

John A. Vitale, AIA, NCARB

Mrs. Alexander J. Walt

W.K. Kellogg Foundation

Beth Yorke, AIA, Past President Detroit 2005

Michigan Architectural Foundation

The mission of the Michigan Architectural Foundation is to increase public appreciation of how architecture enriches life. The Foundation is involved in many worthy endeavors to bring architecture to the public, including publications, scholarships, public education, historic preservation, and elementary school education programs.

For more information, contact

Michigan Architectural Foundation
553 East Jefferson Avenue
Detroit, Michigan 48226
(313) 965-4100

www.michiganarchitecturalfoundation.org
info@michiganarchitecturalfoundation.org

2008 Board of Directors

Timothy A. Casai, FAIA
Randy L. Case, AIA
Ralph Graham, Honorary Affiliate, AIA Michigan
Jeffrey J. Hausman, AIA
Dennis M. King, FAIA
Douglas W. Kueffner, AIA
Phillip Lundwall, FAIA
Ben Maibach III
Michael A. Marshburn, AIA
Thomas R. Mathison, FAIA

Gail McClure
Cynthia Radecki, AIA
Carl D. Roehling, FAIA
Michelle Saroki
Brenda L. Schneider, Honorary Affiliate, AIA Detroit
Park Smith, AIA
Leslie D. Tincknell, FAIA
Albert J. Vegter, AIA

Rae Dumke, Honorary AIA, Executive Director

Made in Michigan

Great Architecture of Michigan was written, photographed, designed, printed, bound, and its paper produced entirely in the state of Michigan.

Protecting our environment is as important as protecting our architectural heritage. Therefore, *Great Architecture of Michigan* is printed on Lustro Offset Environmental (LOE), an elemental chlorine-free paper made using sustainable forestry techniques and including 30% post-consumer waste. Additionally, one hundred percent of the electricity used to manufacture LOE at Sappi Paper's Muskegon Mill is Green-e certified renewable energy.